Enchantment of South America

ARGENTINA

by ALLAN CARPENTER

Consulting Editor
Juan Bouquet, Chancellor
Argentine Consulate, Chicago, Illinois

 CHILDRENS PRESS, CHICAGO

ACKNOWLEDGMENTS

His Excellency Alvaro C. Alsogaray, Ambassador to the United States; Embassy of the Republica Argentina, Washington, D.C.; Argentine Consulate, Chicago, Illinois; Roque Luis DiSabato, Executive Director, Argentine-American Educational Foundation, Chicago, Illinois; Direccion Nacional de Turismo, Buenos Aires, Argentina; Kenneth C. Turner, Photograph Librarian, Pan American Union; Braniff International; Jorge Dubin; Tom Balow.

Map Artist—Eugene Derdeyn
Cover Photograph: Gauchos in Argentina, FPG
Frontispiece: Sunset Over Buenos Aires, Dana Brown, Alpha
Page 6 Photograph: Monument to the Army of the Andes in Mendoza
    atop the "Hill of Glory," P. Gridley, FPG

CONTENTS

A True Story to Set the Scene

"Soldiers! This is the first independent flag to be blessed on this continent. Swear to die in the defense of this flag as I swear it."

"We swear it! Long live our country!" came the cry from five thousand throats.

The man who raised the flag of the Army of the Andes and called for support from the soldiers was Argentine General José de San Martín. He was soon to become one of the world's greatest leaders in the fight for human freedom.

The year was 1817 and the scene was a dramatic one. The soldiers, in full dress uniforms, and most of the citizens of Mendoza were gathered in the main square of the city on the eastern slopes of the Andes Mountains. Banners and pennants fluttered from buildings, and the streets were decorated with flowers. But in spite of the color, the noise, and the enthusiasm of the people,

everyone knew that terrible trials lay ahead.

For three years General San Martín had been preparing for this day. He had long believed that if the United Provinces of La Plata (now Argentina) were to achieve independence from Spain it would be necessary to attack Peru, the center of Spanish power. San Martín believed there was one way the Spanish could be defeated, and he devised a daring plan.

Upon being made governor of the province of Cuyo three years before, San Martín had taken up residence at Mendoza, the provincial capital. Here he had gone ahead with his plan.

General San Martín intended to march an army across the mighty Andes Mountains to meet the Spanish on the western side. Most military experts considered this to be impossible, for it would be difficult for even a few men to cross the Andes passes. How could an entire army do it? General San Martín, however, spent months in making careful preparations.

The people of Mendoza had faith in him and worked very hard to help him create an Army of the Andes. "Men of wealth gave money and rich women their jewels; the poor gave their labor; farmers contributed produce and pack animals—so necessary later to transport supplies over the Andes. A Franciscan priest of Mendoza, Fray Luis Beltran . . . taught the workmen of Cuyo to make cannon, gunpowder, bayonets, saddles, knapsacks, and shoes. He designed special wagons to carry supplies through the narrow passes of the Andes, and made bridges to be thrown across rivers.

"While the men were busy at many kinds of work, the women of Cuyo, led by San Martín's devoted wife, wove cloth, dyed it blue, and made uniforms for the army."

Then, on July 9, 1816, the United Provinces issued a formal Declaration of Independence. The blue and white banner of revolution was unfurled, and Juan Martin de Pueyrredón was named supreme director.

San Martín, knowing the time for action was near, hurried to confer with Pueyrredón. He told him of his plan to conquer Chile and Peru. "It is not the opposition which the royalists can offer to my soldiers . . . but the passage of these immense mountains that will be most troublesome," San Martín declared. Trusting in San Martín, Pueyrredón gave his support and made San Martín captain general of the Army of the Andes.

In 1817 everything was ready. The army had portable bridges with which to cross mountain streams, sleds to carry heavy equipment, and thousands of horseshoes to keep their animals' hooves from slipping on the rocks. Dried beef had been ground into powder that would make a good soup when mixed with corn flour and hot water, and each soldier could carry an eight-day supply. San Martín felt confident that his men could accomplish the unbelievable task ahead of them.

As the long column of men and animals climbed higher and higher into the mountains, trees and flowers disappeared. Only a few cactus plant and moss gave color to the jagged rocks. The only life seen was the lonely, magnificent condor gliding through the sky high above them. The icy summits of the mountains seemed to press down upon the army. The mightiest mountain of them all, Aconcagua, looked like a sentinel whose job it was to keep them out.

For eighteen days the army struggled hard to cross the world's second highest mountain range. They had to cross heights of more than twelve thousand feet where the trails were little wider than ribbons. The bitterly cold winds blew steadily and brought storms of hail or snow.

San Martín and his officers constantly helped the men and cheered them on. Although some six thousand mules and twelve hundred horses died in falls over the rocks or froze to death, the well-equipped and warmly clothed men survived the ordeal.

In one of the greatest feats in military history, San Martín and his faithful, cou-

General José de San Martín and his Army of the Andes struggle over one of the treacherous mountain passes they had to cross in 1817 in order to reach Chile and liberate the country from the Spanish.

rageous men made their way through Los Patos and Uspallata passes, sighted the enemy, and prepared for battle.

They won a great victory at the Battle of Chacabuco in February, 1817. At the Battle of Maipú, in April, 1819, he again defeated the Spanish, liberating Chile from Spanish rule. In July, 1821, San Martín entered the city of Lima and captured the greatest of all Spanish strongholds— Peru. With Spanish power finally broken, the United Provinces no longer needed to fear this constant threat to their independence.

General San Martín had played a key role in setting the whole continent of South America free from Spain. He showed that he lived by his favorite motto: *Serás lo que hay que ser o no eres nada* (You will be what you have to be or nothing). The people of Argentina could ask for no better hero than their fellow countryman who had such foresight, skill, bravery, kindness, patience, and determination.

Five Children of Argentina

Marcelo, Laura, Braulio, Jorge, and Carmen are all Argentines, yet they live widely different kinds of lives because they live in different parts of the country and belong to different families. Marcelo is rich, and Braulio is poor, the others are somewhere in between. Argentina has some extremely wealthy people and some extremely poor people, but the greatest number of people make a comfortable living and are known as the "middle class." Argentina has one of the highest standards of living of any South American country and its people are among the best educated and the healthiest. Here are the stories of five of its young citizens.

MARCELO OF BUENOS AIRES

Marcelo's family is one of "The Two Hundred," the most aristocratic, elegant, influential, and wealthy families of Argentina. His family's wealth came originally from their great *viñedo* in Mendoza Province, where they have grown grapes for many generations. The family also has many other financial interests and investments. They have been wealthy for so long that they do not think much about it.

Marcelo's father spends little time on the family's estate, visiting it only occasionally to consult with his foremen and other workers. He usually takes the whole family with him on these visits. They stay in their "country" residence on the estate, a very large and luxurious house in the old ranch style.

At home in Buenos Aires, Marcelo lives in the town house where his family has lived for generations. Many wealthy Argentine families have given up their rather out of fashion town houses, and prefer to live in the elegant suburbs of the city. Marcelo's father, however, does not wish to give up the house in which he grew up. Marcelo's family also owns a beautiful modern house on the beach at Mar del Plata, where they spend much of the resort season swimming, yachting, golfing, playing tennis, and visiting with their rich friends in the exclusive clubs. Marcelo's father once took him to the great casino, where they gambled a small amount of money.

As is often true in Argentina, relatives other than Marcelo's mother and father live together in the family home. His grandmother, her older brother, an unmarried aunt, two cousins who were orphaned, and Marcelo's married brother and his wife also share the town house.

Marcelo likes most to travel. His father has taken him to the United States, to Paris, to Australia, to Brazil, and often to Uruguay. Marcelo loves to fly into Buenos Aires at sunset when the Río de la Plata shimmers in the last rays of the sun. Seeing this, he understands why it is called the "River of Silver."

As the plane descends toward Ezeiza Airport, it sweeps over the rows of skyscrapers and apartment buildings, gleaming

The Plaza Britannia in Buenos Aires, with the clock tower given to the city by British residents, is one of the many city plazas that Marcelo likes so well.

ALPHA

11

gold and pink in the sunset. The plazas and parks that Marcelo knows so well are almost lost in darkness.

Marcelo loves "his" city and thinks the 450-foot-wide street called Avenida Nueve de Julio is the most exciting place in the world. He sometimes uses his father's charge account at the huge Harrod's Department Store, but his favorite shop is the Iriberri Music Store. Here he adds to his collection of gaucho recordings—the songs of the Argentina cowboys.

Marcelo has gone to opera performances at the Teatro Colón. He likes the museums of Buenos Aires better than those of any other city he has visited. He also likes *futbol,* as soccer is called, better than American baseball or football. He saw a baseball game once in New York, but he does not understand it very well. He thinks American football is slow and not very exciting compared to soccer.

Marcelo feels that he is now old enough to try a *piropo*. This is the old custom of paying a very flowery compliment to a pretty girl as she walks down the street. But he hasn't been brave enough to try and is afraid that his father wouldn't like it. Although the custom is dying, it interests Marcelo more and more.

Marcelo fears to try some things because of *papelón*, the fear of being laughed at. To be the subject of a joke is something that the proud people of Buenos Aires try hard to avoid.

Marcelo does not go to school but is taught by private tutors. He will probably study at the National University of Buenos Aires before finishing his university work in Paris. Marcelo's grandfather studied law in Paris. He used to tell Marcelo of the fascinating things he had seen and done in Paris and how much the French people liked the wealthy young men from Argentina. Marcelo's father had not been able to study in France because of World War II, and this had disappointed him very much.

The family entertains often, mostly at home. When they occasionally take their guests out, they may go to the elegant Alvear Palace Grill or have pepper steaks at the Plaza Hotel, the most fashionable in Argentina. The most socially prominent place is the aristocratic Jockey Club, of which most of Argentina's "first" families are members. Marcelo has been there many times for, of course, his father belongs to the club.

LAURA OF TUCUMÁN

Laura's family owns a vegetable farm near the city of Tucumán. Some of Laura's ancestors came from the Coya Indian tribe. Because she is of mixed Indian and Caucasian blood, Laura is known as a *mestizo*.

Laura loves the small, old elementary school she goes to, even though it lacks modern equipment. When Laura finishes elementary school, she hopes to go on to *colegio*. If she finishes her work at colegio, she will be at the level of a college sophomore in the United States. Then she will be ready to begin her professional training. Laura hopes to be a teacher and dreams of teaching in the university.

A sugar plantation near the city of Tucamán. The great irrigated sugarcane fields of the region where Laura lives have given it the name "Garden of the Republic."

If Laura finishes colegio she will go to the University of Tucumán. If she does not go to colegio, she will go to normal school, where she will prepare to be a primary schoolteacher.

Laura's father is not wealthy. His plantation is small, but he works hard, and irrigation water supplied to his fields helps him grow a good crop.

The city of Tucumán fascinates Laura, although the bustle of its traffic almost frightens this girl from the country. Most of all she likes the Casa Histórica, where her country made its declaration of independence.

Laura also likes the monument to General Belgrano, one of the heroes of the Argentine war for independence, and knows by heart all the words on this monument. Another of her favorite heroes is Bishop Colombres, who brought to the region the first wooden press for crushing sugarcane. She has visited the museum where this press is exhibited.

For Laura the highlight of the year is the Festival of the Sugar Harvest at Tucumán in October. She likes the music concerts and the art shows, but most of all she dreams that some day she may be elected "Sugar Queen."

BRAULIO OF PATAGONIA

Braulio loves all the animals on the large *estancia* (ranch) where his father is one of the shepherds. Braulio especially loves the eager and intelligent sheep dogs, so highly trained they almost seem human. The owner of the ranch came to Argentina from England. He leases nearly 50,000 acres of land from the government and owns several thousand acres more where he keeps thousands of sheep. For all this land he hires only twelve shepherds, but has almost sixty dogs to do much of the work of guarding and herding the sheep.

Braulio's family lives in a small but very neat house supplied by the ranch owner.

13

Their home is not far from the town of José de San Martín, almost in the shadow of the Andes Mountains that mark the border between Argentina and Chile in the part of Argentina known as Patagonia.

Braulio and the other children of the shepherds attend classes in one of the ranch buildings. Here they are taught by the wife of the ranch owner, who once was a teacher in England. Braulio probably will not go further than elementary school.

If he did not love the outdoors so much, life might be dull for Braulio. But he likes to watch the many birds and listen to their calls. He has often gazed in awe at the magnificent condor flying high above him. Braulio has made friends with many of the small wild animals of the neighborhood. Occasionally he sees a deer, and once he had the good luck to spot a great red stag.

Braulio would like to be a trainer and keeper of the sheep dogs. He studies the way the dogs are trained to do their difficult work of herding and guarding the sheep. Sometimes he goes with his father to the lonely fields where several acres are needed to provide grazing for just one sheep. There he is allowed to work the dogs.

The most exciting times on the estancia come when the sheep are sheared. The expert shearers can strip off as much as ten pounds of wool from a healthy animal.

Sheep that are to be sold for meat must be shipped to the *frigorifico*—the meat packing plant. Braulio hopes that soon he will be allowed to go on one of the trips to the frigorifico.

JORGE OF CÓRDOBA

Jorge is a *Cordobés,* a resident of Córdoba. His father is an executive in Kaiser Industries, the United States manufacturer that established an automobile manufacturing plant at Córdoba. Jorge's father was one of the first native-born Argentine men to become an automobile executive. When the automobile industry first came to Argentina, there were very few Argentine men who knew how to manufacture cars. Auto executives had to come from the United States, Germany, Italy, and France.

Braulio's family lives near the foothills of the Andes, in an area of Patagonia much like this one.

JORGE DUBIN

14

An example of the beautiful Spanish colonial architecture in Jorge's home city of Córdoba.

However, the automobile manufacturers began to train the Argentines so that now the automobile factories are managed almost entirely by them. Jorge's father and his family are fortunate. His income is high enough to support his family very comfortably. Jorge has several friends whose fathers have to work at two, and even three, jobs to earn enough money to support their families. This is due to the great rise in the cost of living because of inflation.

Jorge's mother is a descendant of a very old Spanish family of Córdoba. His father's grandfather came from Italy soon after the beginning of the century. Jorge and his family live in a comfortable modern home in one of the better and newer districts of Córdoba. They also own a cottage on the blue lake that was formed by the San Roque Dam across the Río Primero. Jorge loves to water-ski, swim, and sail when the family goes to the cottage.

Jorge's principal hobby is wood carving. The great Cathedral of Córdoba, other churches in the city, and many buildings of Córdoba University have fine wood carvings inside. These were done by Indian artists who had been taught by the Jesuit priests and brought into the region for their skills. A descendant of one of the Indian artists lives in Córdoba and still carries on the wood-carving tradition of his ancestors. He teaches wood carving and other crafts to a small group of talented students, which includes Jorge. Jorge won third place for a wood sculpture that he entered in the Kaiser art exhibition, which is held every two years. While his teacher thinks he should become an artist, Jorge does not want to make art his life work.

Jorge is proud of the skyscrapers of ten and twelve stories that are rising in Córdoba. In spite of this, he would like his beautiful city to continue to look much as it did in Spanish colonial days with its handsome cathedral, viceroy's house, and the ancient Cabildo—the colonial town hall.

15

Jorge's school is one of the newest and best equipped in Córdoba. The teachers are excellent; many of them are graduates of the university. The school has a good library, fine textbooks, audiovisual materials, and other new teaching tools.

Because Jorge is a good student, he plans to complete colegio and continue his work at the University of Córdoba. This is one of the oldest universities in the Western Hemisphere, and it now has nearly twenty thousand students and a large faculty. Jorge is not interested in attending a university in France or America, although he could do so if he wished.

With thirteen national holidays to celebrate each year, Jorge and his father have time for their favorite sport. They love to hunt on the estancia of a friend who lives near the small town of Jesus Maria, about thirty-two miles from Córdoba. Here the wild goats and foxes provide plentiful game.

Jorge and his family also like to drive up into the Córdoba range of mountains. One of Jorge's favorite spots is the small lake on the very top of Champagui, the highest mountain in the range.

CARMEN OF MISIONES

Carmen lives with her parents in the province of Misiones in the small city of Puerto Mineral on the great Paraná River. Her father is a physician, and they live comfortably in a large old house surrounded by beautiful trees and flowers that grow wild in this semitropical land.

In the cedar and pine forests outside the city, monkeys swing from the trees and water hogs and large tapir roam the underbrush. The great cats—the snarling puma and the ferocious jaguar—slink silently through the forests. Overhead flit jungle birds like the raucous parrots and toucans whose enormous brightly colored beaks look as if they were painted by an artist.

Carmen goes to a very good Catholic school in Puerto Mineral. The building is old, but the nuns are well educated, fond of children, and devoted to teaching them. Carmen's parents do not plan to send their daughter to the university. They would like her to marry, as most of the girls of the area have already done. Carmen, however, has different ideas. She wants to become an archaeologist. Since her grades are good and she is persistent, her parents will probably see that she gets the education she needs.

Carmen became interested in archaeology when she and her family visited San Ignacio Mini, the ruins of an Indian town established by the Jesuits. After it was deserted and fell into decay, it was covered by the jungle. Now it has been uncovered and made into a national historic site. As the family looked through the streets of the ruined town, Carmen could see the work that the experts had done in clearing the brush away from the streets and buildings and uncovering the thick stone walls that were still standing. Only the roofs are missing, and these may one day be restored.

Carmen was fascinated by the thought of discovering and uncovering ancient cities

Iguazú Falls, the breathtaking sight that Carmen saw when she was there on a trip with her family.

and buildings and finding items once used by the people who had lived there. When she went home, she read everything she could about such work and decided that this was what she wanted to do.

Carmen had another exciting trip when her family made the journey to Iguazú Falls, more than a hundred miles upriver from Puerto Mineral. Higher and wider than Niagara Falls, Iguazú Falls is one of the top natural wonders of the world. The family stayed overnight at the Hotel Cataratas de Argentina, only about a thousand feet from the falls. They took the trip partly by rowboat and partly over wooden footwalks that go into the falls—an exciting moment for the entire family. The roar of the falls, the rush of the water, the spray of foam, and the rainbows shining in the spray thrilled Carmen.

On the way home, the family visited the birthplace of the Argentine hero of independence, José de San Martín. In the little town of Yapeyú, the government has built a fine museum to enclose the ruined walls of the house where San Martín was born. Carmen thinks San Martín was one of the greatest men who ever lived.

Her father has promised that some day the family will go by boat several days' journey down the Paraná River and visit Buenos Aires. Carmen can hardly wait.

A Land of Many Faces

The eighth largest country in the world, and the second largest country in South America, Argentina is a spectacular land of many contrasts. It has jungles teeming with wild animals; it has frozen wastes where penguins waddle. It has lofty mountains and endless flatlands. It has cold blue lakes at the foot of glaciers, and places where there are no lakes for hundreds of miles and where even rivers disappear. It is a land of tropical heat, yet it also has a region of bitter cold. A land of many faces, Argentina has been called one of the loveliest countries on earth.

All of Argentina lies farther east than New York City. The country is "long,"

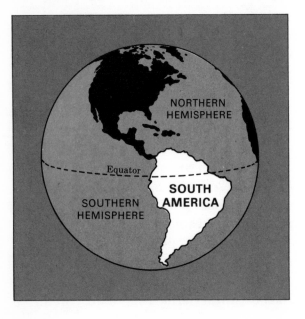

stretching for 2,295 miles from north to south. Although it covers an area about one-third the size of the United States, its greatest distance from east to west is only 980 miles. It is bordered on the north by Bolivia and Paraguay; on the east by Brazil, Uruguay, and the Atlantic Ocean; and on the west by Chile. The coast of Argentina, stretching for 1,600 miles, ends at the tip of the continent where South America dips into the frigid waters of the Antarctic.

As the United States is divided into states with the District of Columbia as a separate unit, so is Argentina divided into twenty-two provinces, with a separate Federal Capital District. It has one territory, Tierra del Fuego, in the far south, separated from the mainland by the Strait of Magellan.

While Argentina claims a part of the Antarctic continent reaching to the South Pole, Chile disputes this claim. The matter has not yet been settled. Ownership of the faraway, barren Falkland Islands is also claimed by Argentina, though they are governed by Great Britain and are generally recognized as a British Crown Colony.

As early as 1602, a Spanish poet, Centenera, had called the land *Argentina,* from the Latin word *argentum* (silver), but the name did not become official until 1860. The idea of silver came from the name of the Río de la Plata, which means "River of Silver" in Spanish. There are many different explanations of why the river came to be known as the river of

PROVINCES OF ARGENTINA

silver. One is that the early explorers hoped it would lead them to a land rich in silver. Another is that at certain times the water of this great wide river shines like silver.

FOUR MAIN REGIONS

Most of Argentina is a great plain, sloping toward the sea from the heights of the Andes Mountains. However, the country contains four main geographical or physical areas. The heart of the country is the flat plain known as the *Pampa*. The other regions fan out from the Pampa—the northern lowlands, the Andes Mountain region to the west (the *Andine*), and another enormous plain in southern Argentina known as *Patagonia*.

The word *pampa* means "plain," or "prairie." This area is much like the Great Plains in the United States. The pampas seem to stretch out for limitless miles without trees or anything else appearing on the horizon. It is possible to drive for more than a hundred miles and not cross a stream. Fanning out from Buenos Aires for three or four hundred miles, the plains cover about a fourth of the entire country. Some of the richest soil in the world is found in the pampas. Although the early explorers thought it was a wilderness, today two-thirds of the people of Argentina make their living from this important region.

Patagonia, south of the Pampa, occupies another fourth of the country. This dry, often rocky, region supports only about three percent of the entire population.

The northernmost region has three sections. In the center is the Gran Chaco, a subtropical land of forests with much wildlife. In the west is the Puna, a high, level area with fine forests of hardwood trees. Here, crops grow well on the cleared lands. The rolling foothills of the mountains are dry but can be farmed with irrigation. Many minerals are also found in the mountains. The attraction of this region is its great beauty. In the east is a swampy, forested area known as Mesopotamia, after the Biblical land. This area, which lies between the Paraná and Uruguay rivers, is often flooded.

"FATHER OF WATERS"

One of the great water systems of the world empties into the Río de la Plata, which is not really a river. Actually, it is the mouth of an ancient river and its valley. These sank below the sea in ancient times and became an arm of the sea, known as an *estuary*. Into this estuary pours the great flood of water from the Paraná and Uruguay rivers.

The Guaraní Indians called the river *Paraná,* which means "Father of Waters" in their language, just as Mississippi meant "Father of Waters" to Indians in the United States. As far north as Posadas, the Paraná is still a mile and a half wide and forms the border between Argentina and southeastern Paraguay. The Paraguay River forms another section of the boundary between these two countries.

A tributary of the Paraguay River, the Pilcomayo, forms the rest of the great river

boundary between Paraguay and Argentina. This river runs between northern Argentina and Paraguay. About halfway across, it unexpectedly splits. Its northern part flows into Paraguay and is known as the Confuso. This name probably stands for "confusion" because of the split. The southern portion of the Pilcomayo River continues the border east to where it meets the Paraguay River at the city of Asunción in Paraguay.

Another river boundary is formed by the great Uruguay River. This flows between the countries of Uruguay and Argentina. It also empties into the Río de la Plata.

Many Argentine rivers never reach the sea. The Salado is the only large river that flows across the entire Pampa region. Several rivers flow into Mar Chiquita, a large salty lake with no outlet to the sea. Another salt and mineral lake is Lake Epecuén near Carhué. This lake has twenty times more salt than the ocean. Its waters are popular for treating skin diseases.

MOUNTAIN MIRRORS

One of the world's most beautiful lakes is Lake Nahuel Huapí. This is one of the many lakes that border the Andes Mountains on both sides from Nequén Province through Tierra del Fuego. Some of these lakes cut across the international boundary line and are shared with Chile.

The other principal mountain lakes (*lago* in Spanish) include Lago Buenos Aires, Lago Posadas, Lago San Martín, Lago Viedma, Lago Argentino, and Lago Fagnano. The last stretches for sixty-five miles across the island of Tierra del Fuego.

There are some smaller lakes in northern Patagonia, but in the rest of Argentina few lakes are found. Some lakes exist only during rainy seasons or at high water.

Argentina has lagged behind other countries in damming rivers to make artificial lakes. However, there are some artificial lakes and more are being built or planned.

MAGNIFICENT MOUNTAINS

The mountains that run down the west coast of both the Americas reach their loftiest and most magnificent heights on the border of Chile and Argentina. The two highest mountains in the hemisphere lie within Argentina. Awe-inspiring, gigantic Mount Aconcagua soars to a height of 22,834 feet. Of the fourteen highest mountains of South America, all but two touch Argentina or lie entirely within its borders. Only a little lower than Aconcagua is Mercedario, 22,211 feet high.

The most easterly part of the Andes of Argentina is the Sierra de Córdoba, called the Córdoba Hills. This range is made up of three groups of small mountains. The highest, Mount Champaquí at 8,451 feet, has a small lake at the very top. The Sierras stretch for about three hundred miles from north to south and are ninety miles wide.

THE ANCIENT LAND

The bedrock under the pampas is said to be one of the oldest land masses on

The peak of Mount Aconcagua, 22,834 feet high, is hidden by clouds in this impressive photograph of the Andes Mountains in Argentina.

earth. Throughout time, soil has been washed and blown from the mountains to cover this ancient bedrock. Land formed in this way is known as alluvial land. At Buenos Aires the alluvial soil is almost a thousand feet deep. Most lands of the Chaco were also formed in this way.

The Andes are considered young for mountains because they appeared not more than 100,000,000 years ago. Enormous forces beneath the earth began to push up these great blocks of the earth's surface. Over millions of years the surface continued to rise until the Andes loomed almost the length of the continent. The steepest rise was on the western side, and the Andes sloped down to the east. Since they were formed, the Andes have been shaped, molded, and smoothed by the action of wind, water, and frost.

23

However, the greatest sculptors of the land were the mighty glaciers. Beginning about 50,000,000 years ago the world turned colder. Snow piled up thousands of feet thick, becoming solid ice. These great masses of ice slid along slowly, changing the land in their path. As the climate again grew warmer, they gradually melted. This happened four times.

In Argentina the glaciers blocked the rivers, reversed their flows, and even changed the location of the continental divide. When the glaciers melted, the tremendous flow of water cut through the land, forming deep canyons that slash across Patagonia.

Most of the lakes of Argentina's lake region were left by the glaciers. Some lie in deep holes chiseled out by the force of the ice. Others were formed when rivers were dammed by earth and rock. Such dams are called *moraines*.

There are still glaciers in the mountains of Argentina. Some of these come down to the glacial lakes. Some, such as Moreno Glacier on Lago Viedma, still form icebergs. Huge chunks of the glacier drop into the lake with a roar to become gleaming blue-white islands of ice. This process is called "calving." Many of the glaciers are growing smaller, but Moreno is one that continues to grow bigger.

Heat and fire changed other parts of Argentina. The Paraná Plateau of the Misiones area is thought to be formed of lava. This red-hot rock must have flowed over the land in tremendous quantities at some ancient time. Today this rock is known for its extreme hardness.

Argentina is not especially known for its fossils, which are objects or traces of animals and plants of past ages. However, one of the most interesting fossil areas of Argentina is the Bosque Petrificado. This national park preserves one of the world's most remarkable petrified forests. The stony remains of some araucaria trees found there are more than ten feet around; the remains of some of the trunks are more than seventy feet long. The trees are thought to be about 70,000 years old.

TOPSY-TURVY CLIMATE

January is the hottest month in Buenos Aires; June, July, and August are the winter months. The reason is that Argentina lies across much of the middle part of the Southern Hemisphere, where the seasons are the opposite of those in the Northern Hemisphere.

Most of the temperate part of South America is found within Argentina. The country is so long, however, that its climate ranges from great cold to great heat—from a subarctic to a subtropic climate. The Argentine Chaco has had the highest

Lake Nahuel Haupí, one of the many lakes in Argentina's lake region that were formed by the force of moving glaciers.
MOORE MC CORMACK LINES

The city of Ushuaia is on the island of Tierra del Fuego, the southernmost point in Argentina. Antarctica is only six hundred miles to the south.

temperature ever recorded anywhere in South America. Temperate Argentina has moderate, pleasant temperatures.

As the visitor goes farther south, he finds the weather growing cooler. If Argentina's claims to Antarctica are ever recognized, the country will be able to boast of some of the coldest temperatures in the world.

RAINFALL

The eastern pampas have the most rain —thirty-six to thirty-nine inches a year. At the western edge of the pampas the rainfall is barely twenty inches per year. Three-fourths of Argentina is dry—arid or semi-arid. Most of Patagonia is arid, with winter snows providing most of the moisture. The eastern part of Patagonia is nearly desert, while Misiones Province is a subtropical rain forest.

The pampas are known for their violent storms. When heavy rains come to the pampas or to the Chaco regions, the land is so flat that the water cannot drain off quickly.

Yesterday and Today

The first European ship ever to sail into the River of Silver was that of Spanish explorer Juan Díaz de Solís in 1516. The discoverer of the land that was to become Argentina claimed the entire great area in the name of the king of Spain. However, he and most of his followers were killed by Indians.

Later, the great navigator Ferdinand Magellan made the Spanish claim stronger. He sailed down the coast in 1520 and discovered the water passage between the Atlantic and Pacific oceans that was to bear his name—the Strait of Magellan. He was one of many explorers who tried to find a way to get through the New World to the Pacific Ocean. This passageway is so far south and the seas so stormy, however, that it did not prove to be as useful as the one that would later cut across the center of the Western Hemisphere.

FERDINAND MAGELLANUS.

Other explorers continued to look for an easier passage between the Atlantic and Pacific oceans. They also looked eagerly for the mountains of silver and gold that they had heard about in stories. Determined to find these riches, Sebastian Cabot in 1527 set up Fort Sancti Spiritus, north of present-day Rosario, and sent explorers looking for the famous silver mountain of the Incas. It always seemed only a short distance away, but they never found it. They did, however, decide to name the river the River of Silver—Río de la Plata.

The largest expedition that had ever sailed to the New World arrived at the River of Silver in February of 1536. The huge force—more than two thousand men and one hundred horses in eleven ships—was led by the great Spanish nobleman, Pedro de Mendoza. He planned to establish a colony that would be a base from which the country could be explored. Finding a small stream emptying into the Plata, he set up his colony there and named it Nuestra Señora Santa María del Buen Aire, for the Virgin Mary, Patroness of the navigator. This first settlement on the site of Buenos Aires was to give the city its name, meaning "fair winds."

The settlers' supplies grew scarce and new supplies failed to arrive from Spain. To add to the settlers' troubles, the Querandí Indians attacked the settlement. These were the first Indians the Spaniards had met in the New World who were not afraid of horses. The Indians shot their fiery arrows into the settlement, setting fire to the thatched roofs of the Spaniards' homes.

They kept up a fearless siege until the Spanish were completely out of food and were finally forced to eat snakes, rats, and even the soles of their shoes. Discouraged by Indian attacks and quite ill, Mendoza sailed for Spain and died on the way.

Those of his followers who stayed behind went farther up the river and established settlements in what is now Paraguay. The first "Buenos Aires" had failed in less than five years.

A FIRM FOOTHOLD

One of the strangest facts about Argentine history is that the first permanent towns were founded far inland by settlers who came across the rugged mountains from the Spanish-held lands of Peru. Not until much later were permanent towns built along the easily reached riverfronts near the east coast. The oldest city on Argentine soil is Santiago del Estero, founded in 1553 on the west bank of the Río Dulce. Mendoza, founded in 1561; San Juan a year later; Tucumán in 1582 (but not at its present location); Córdoba, 1573; Salta, 1582; Corrientes, 1588; La Rioja, 1591; and Jujuy, 1593, were other early settlements. All are thriving today.

A typical town was laid out like a Spanish city. The leaders chose a place which was near a good water supply and which could be defended against hostile Indians. They set out a central plaza with streets in rectangles around it. Every community was dedicated in a colorful ceremony in which the townspeople asked the

Sebastian Cabot searched for the legendary silver mountain of the Incas.

PAN AMERICAN UNION

blessing of God the Father, the Son, and the Holy Ghost, of the Virgin Mary, of many saints, and of the king. The new towns depended on friendly Indians for their labor supply. Most of the Indians worked under the control of local leaders in a kind of forced labor.

One of the most successful founders of cities was Captain Juan de Garay, who established Santa Fe in 1573. Seven years later he set up a new community on the Río de la Plata where the ill-fated fort of Mendoza had stood. This community was the beginning of what is now the city of Buenos Aires.

During the early years, most of the settlements had a hard time surviving. Goods had to be carried over the narrow, difficult mountain passes from Peru and even more distant Panama. The Indians of the coast were fiercer, which made living in the interior easier and safer. At that time Spain would not permit Buenos Aires or other coastal towns to trade directly with countries across the Atlantic. While trading was done from Buenos Aires, this was illegal smuggling. For these reasons the coast towns did not grow rapidly during this period.

MEN OF MISSION

Most of the Guaraní Indians lived peacefully with the Spaniards along the Paraná River. With the help of the Jesuit missionaries, some of the most unusual and successful Indian towns in the Western Hemisphere were set up. The first Jesuit mission community in Argentina was founded in 1617. Less than a hundred years later there were fifteen Jesuit mission towns in Argentina. San Ignacio Mini had a population of 4,356 in 1731 when it hit its peak. Today's province of Misiones takes its name from these early missions.

The Jesuits taught the Guaraní Indians how to improve their farming methods. They developed a flourishing industry in *yerba maté,* a kind of tea, sometimes called Jesuit tea. During this period the Indians lived as comfortably as do many modern Argentine families. Almost every family had its own plot of land with good houses of sturdy stone construction. All Indian children went to schools, and most of them were educated through what is high school today. They were taught many subjects— art, music, and even Latin.

Hospitals, homes for orphans and widows, and homes for the aged all were operated by the Indians themselves with the help of Jesuit priests. No Spanish residents were permitted in the mission communities. The Indians governed themselves, electing a mayor, called an *alcalde,* and other officers. Only the men could vote, and voting took place whenever the town needed to decide something.

The ruins of San Ignacio Mini, one of the Argentine Jesuit mission towns that flourished between 1617 and 1767.

Together, the Indians and the Jesuits built a truly remarkable civilization in the wilderness. The Indians learned printing and built fine churches and artistic buildings. Sometimes they presented grand opera, singing it in its original language.

When Spanish settlers became jealous of the Jesuit Indian missions, they told the King of Spain that the Jesuits had found rich mines of silver and were concealing them. In 1767, King Charles III ordered all Jesuits out and placed many of them in prison. Many Indians fled into the jungle to escape being taken into slavery, and the rich civilization became a memory of the past.

VICEROYALTY OF THE RÍO DE LA PLATA

The population of the country increased slowly. Buenos Aires had a population of 1,000 in 1600 and only 8,000 in 1750. Córdoba was the same size. Tucumán had grown from 2,000 to 7,000 in the same period. Shops, offices, stores, warehouses, and churches had sprung up in towns across the country. Some streets were now paved with cobblestones. In the country, huge estancias, the estates of the wealthy Spanish, began to flourish. Some of these were as large as a million acres.

Tucumán lay on the main route of travel to the mines of Bolivia and Peru. The region was noted for rice and cotton and the manufacture of huge lumbering oxcarts. Many mules also were raised here. The largest mule market in the empire of Spain was at Salta, for mules were used in the mines there. Santiago del Estero manufactured large quantities of cloth. The eastern towns lived mainly by smuggling and raising horses, mules, and cattle.

Little attention was paid to the Buenos Aires region until 1776. In that year Spain created the Viceroyalty of the Río de la Plata, with Buenos Aires as its capital. This region included the present countries of Argentina, Bolivia, Paraguay, and Uruguay. It was the last great region to be formed in the Spanish Empire and became equal in rank to the much older viceroyalties of Mexico, Peru, and New Granada.

After almost two hundred years of neglect, the port of Buenos Aires was finally opened to Spanish shipping, and the colony enjoyed its greatest period of prosperity.

In Europe, England and Spain were at war. When the English attacked and captured Buenos Aires in 1806, the Spanish Viceroy fled. The local commander, Santiago de Liniers y Bremond, called together a group of volunteer militiamen and managed to recapture the city. In 1807 another group of British under a General Whitelock again entered the city. This time a citizen army fought so bravely and fiercely that the British were forced to surrender in one of the worst defeats ever suffered by British forces.

Meanwhile, Napoleon Bonaparte had forced the King of Spain to flee his throne. This threw the Spanish colonies into great confusion. Many colonists felt that this gave them the opportunity to declare their independence as the United States had done about thirty years before. People

This lovely home on the estate of an Argentine family is typical
of the homes being built by wealthy Spaniards by the 1750's.

thought that if they could defeat a trained British force, it would be difficult for Spanish forces to keep them under control.

INDEPENDENCE!

On May 25, 1810, a huge throng gathered in the plaza outside the historic cabildo in Buenos Aires. The Viceroy was forced to resign, and a patriotic ruling group called a *junta* was organized with Cornelio Saavedra as president. Two of Argentina's great patriots, Mariano Moreno and Manuel Belgrano, were members of the junta. However, the new leaders declared that they were ruling in the name of the displaced King of Spain.

The new country called itself the United Provinces of La Plata. It boasted a population of 400,000 of which 210,000 were Indians. More than forty years were to pass before the region became a real nation. Soon after the country became independent, the new leaders had to fight the Spanish to establish their freedom. The Viceroy of Peru was ordered to subdue the people of the United Provinces and to bring them back under Spanish rule. One of the earliest battles was the Battle of Tucumán in 1812 that resulted in a victory for the United Provinces. Led by General Manuel Belgrano, the citizens of Tucumán played an important part in the winning of this victory.

The year 1812 also brought one of South America's greatest patriots back to Argentina. José de San Martín returned to his native land after many years in Europe. Some Argentine leaders did not trust him, thinking he might be an undercover man for the Spanish.

San Martín soon proved his loyalty by using his long military experience to train troops for the United Provinces. Before long he had developed one of the world's best-trained regiments. In February, 1813, eleven Spanish ships landed their men in an attack at the Paraná River north of Buenos

This sweeping view of a section of the Andes Mountains shows the treacherous obstacles General San Martín and his army had to overcome in 1817 when they crossed the Andes to attack the Spanish in Chile.

Aires. San Martín and his regiment were ready in the Convent of San Lorenzo. In the furious battle that followed, San Martín's horse was shot from under him and he was almost killed, but he and his men won. This victory proved that San Martín was not a spy but a great patriot. It also demonstrated his tremendous military ability.

TIMES OF TURMOIL

In the following years the United Provinces faced many dangers. The Spanish King Ferdinand VII had regained his throne and was determined to reclaim his lost provinces. The people of the provinces were quarreling among themselves and could not unite. Between 1814 and 1821, General Martín Guëmes fought off seven different efforts of the Spanish to descend on the United Provinces from the northwest. General Güemes, popular hero of the revolution, led forces that were mainly made up of colorful gauchos. Dressed in colorful red costumes, these "cowboys" of Argentina fought wildly and bravely.

General San Martín knew that as long as Spain controlled Chile and Peru, these attacks could continue and the United Provinces would never be safe.

Meanwhile, it seemed as if the government of the United Provinces might fall apart. San Martín, Manuel Belgrano, and other patriots urged a formal declaration of independence from Spain. This declaration would be like the one signed forty years before that resulted in the United States of America.

With the support of the masses of the people, a congress met at Tucumán to write an official declaration. On July 9, 1816, the Congress of Tucumán proclaimed independence for the country that later would be called Argentina.

In 1817, General San Martín led his Army of the Andes across the mountains and attacked the Spanish in Chile. After defeating the Spanish at Chacabuco, San Martín took Santiago. Then in 1820 he invaded Peru, capturing the city of Lima in 1821. After the fall of Lima, Spanish power collapsed. The United Provinces were now in control of their own destiny.

However, peace was not to come to the United Provinces for many years. Leaders were divided into two powerful groups—the Unitarians who wanted a strong central government with headquarters at Buenos Aires, and the Federalists who wanted to keep most of the power in the provinces. These two groups struggled for power for many years. Leaders in the Federalist group were wealthy and powerful men known as *caudillos*. Supported by private armies of gauchos, the caudillos ruled their own areas almost like feudal lords.

After the congress at Buenos Aires had set up a constitution in 1826, Bernardino Rivadavia became the first elected presi-

This painting by Antonio Moreno shows the Congress of Tucumán on July 9, 1816, as independence for the United Provinces was proclaimed.

dent of the United Provinces. The caudillos were so much against a central government that they overthrew Rivadavia. The country was thrown into further confusion and disorder. During the period of 1825-1828, the United Provinces also were at war with Brazil. As a result of this war, Uruguay became a separate nation—a buffer state between Brazil and Argentina.

Juan Manuel de Rosas, governor of Buenos Aires, became more and more powerful. Rosas was the leader of the important group of wealthy estancia owners. They raised herds of cattle whose meat was salted in *saladeros* (salting plants) and sold to Brazil and Cuba. To gain more power, Rosas used secret societies that murdered his enemies or destroyed their property. By 1835 he had become an absolute dictator. The country suffered through a seventeen-year reign of terror.

In 1851 Justo José de Urquiza began to oppose Rosas. A former assistant who had become governor of Entre Ríos Province, Urquiza persuaded Brazil and Uruguay to join his forces. Together they defeated dictator Rosas in the battle of Caseros near Buenos Aires in 1852. Rosas managed to slip out of the country and escaped to England, where he lived in exile for twenty-five years.

UNIFYING THE COUNTRY

Almost immediately after the defeat of Rosas, General Urquiza called a constitutional convention to meet in Santa Fe in 1853 for the purpose of creating a constitu-

Juan Manuel de Rosas, governor of Buenos Aires.

tion much like that of the United States. However, their constitution was more like the Articles of Confederation that did not work in the United States. The new constitution called for a grouping of thirteen provinces (just as there had been thirteen original states in the early Confederation in the United States). In spite of its faults, the new constitution was a great step forward in bringing the country together, although Buenos Aires did not join. On May 25, 1853, Urquiza was elected the first president under the constitution, and Paraná was named the capital.

Buenos Aires Province and the Confederation opposed each other until 1862 when a Buenos Aires man, Bartolomé Mitre, became president. The capital was moved to Buenos Aires, but the federal officials often seemed to be little more than guests of the powerful province of Buenos Aires.

A long war with Paraguay, beginning in 1865, was one of the many difficulties of the period. These troubles included the plagues of cholera and yellow fever in the 1860's and 1870's. Mendoza was almost completely wiped out by an earthquake in 1861.

The Indians still presented one of the greatest problems. Due to Indian threats, land south and west of the Río Salado was unoccupied by European settlers. It was a land much like the western United States, where the Indians were supreme. The Araucanian Indians frequently raided the European settlements, carrying off cattle and horses which they took over the mountains to sell in Chile. A line of forts protected the outer rim of "civilization" from Indian attack. As further protection, the government in the 1870's dug a ten-foot ditch for 240 miles to help guard against Indian attack.

Finally the Ministry of War sent a young army officer, Julio A. Roca, to wipe out the Indians. In a series of battles during 1879 and 1880, Roca and his men fought the Indians relentlessly. When this "Campaign of the Desert" was over, the Indians of Patagonia had been almost completely wiped out.

Roca's military leadership was so admired that after a brief revolution in 1880

he was made president of his country. At this time, the province of Buenos Aires agreed to let the city of Buenos Aires become a federal district. The new national capital was established here, and the country was named Argentina. The province of Buenos Aires was forced to set up a new capital at La Plata.

TOWARD MORE DEMOCRACY

Though control of Argentina continued to be held by a small group of wealthy, educated people, the country began a period of prosperity of a kind it had never known before.

Justo José de Urquíza, first president elected under the constitution of 1853.

Hipólito Irigoyen, elected president in 1916.

The rapid growth of Buenos Aires and other coastal cities attracted nearly a million immigrants from Europe in the 1880's alone. During the following years the middle classes began to emerge and voice their demands for participation in the political affairs of the country. They were not to achieve their goals, however, until 1910, the year Argentina celebrated its first hundred years of independence.

In this year, the distinguished Dr. Roque Sáenz Peña became president. He worked long and hard to make elections honest, to give more people the vote. In 1912 a law was passed giving the vote to all males over eighteen years of age. The ballot was to be secret, and all who were eligible to vote were required to do so. This Sáenz Peña law is considered the turning point in making Argentina a more democratic nation.

The first free national elections were held in 1916, when Hipólito Irigoyen won the presidency by only one electoral vote. During his term, laws were passed favoring workers and people who until then had not been given much consideration.

Argentina remained neutral during World War I. The country's food products were in such great demand that Argentina became very prosperous, with the Argentine peso considered the best currency in the world.

One of the most difficult periods came in 1919 after the war. Labor troubles developed into the "Tragic Week"—in January of that year, when many manufacturing plants were destroyed. Streetcars were burned and there were several shootings. Although the middle class won some political victories, Argentina remained firmly in the hands of the upper class.

After 1922, under the able administration of Marcelo T. de Alvear, who succeeded Irigoyen, the country experienced more prosperity. Irigoyen was elected again in 1928 with a program of social reform and industrial expansion. Because aristocratic Argentines thought he was too liberal, however, Irigoyen was ousted by the army. When José F. Uriburu was installed as president, he suppressed labor unions and the press.

In the election of November, 1931, General Agustín P. Justo was elected president by the Conservatives. Under his leadership, Argentina recovered rapidly from the worldwide depression of the period.

LESS DEMOCRACY

Robert M. Ortiz, in 1937, and Ramón Castillo, in 1942, were the last civilian leaders of Argentina for twelve years. The military leaders took over in 1943.

Argentina faced many problems. World War II had cut off important foreign markets, and both the Axis powers and the Allies wanted Argentine support. For a time it appeared that Argentina might side with Germany and Japan. Pressure from the United States finally brought an Argentine declaration of war against the Axis.

One of the military leaders who had helped to overthrow Castillo in 1943 was Juan Domingo Perón. The power he built as Minister of Labor enabled him to rise swiftly. He was tremendously popular with working people, the *descamisados*, or "Shirtless ones," who called him their "savior."

Perón ran for president in 1946 and won. Even those men who ran against him admitted that this was the most honest and the most free election so far in Argentine history. Perón based his growing power on the rise of the lower classes and appealed to them with oratory and favors. His wife, Eva, organized the country's welfare and became almost a saint to the poor and to the working people. The mixture of fascism and national socialism which Perón put together was called *justicialismo*.

Juan Domingo Perón, president and dictator.

In 1947 the government bought the railroads from England. The wages of workingmen rose; factory workers were given paid vacations; hours became shorter; medical and retirement benefits increased. Perón started housing projects and encouraged manufacture of refrigerators, bicycles, radios, and other products.

However, Perón helped to squander much of the wealth of the country. Agriculture and industry could not keep up with the demands of the working people for more good things with less working time. The cost of living began to rise rapidly. When Eva Perón died in July of 1952, her husband lost his greatest champion.

41

Although he had been reelected in 1951, Perón was forced out by military leaders on September 16, 1955, after a week of fighting in Córdoba, Bahía Blanca, and Mendoza, and the successful blockade of Buenos Aires by the Argentine fleet.

Juan Perón went into exile, but still had a tremendous following in Argentina. After that time, there were many unsuccessful attempts by Perón and his followers to get back into power.

The revolution that overthrew Perón was the first "popular" revolution in Argentine history, with ordinary men and women taking part, not only the aristocracy and army men. Perón lost his power because he became a tyrant, persecuting the church and people who held other views, and even proposing to make a new army of his "Peronista" workers. Army leaders could not let this threat to their power continue.

TURBULENT TIMES

In spite of tremendous difficulties, General Pedro Aramburu governed Argentina wisely for two years. He helped the nation return to democracy with elections in 1958. With the help of Perón's followers, Dr. Arturo Frondizi was elected president. One of his greatest problems was the high rise in the cost of living. By 1963 people had to pay sixty times as much for food and other necessities as they had paid in 1943.

Although Frondizi had accomplished much for his country, the armed forces overthrew him on March 29, 1962. He had reduced the danger of inflation, fired almost 200,000 unneeded government employees, turned over many poorly managed government businesses to private owners, allowed new machinery to be imported, increased the collection of taxes, built roads and power plants, and improved Buenos Aires.

Following Frondizi, the head of the Argentine Senate, José Maria Guido, took over until Dr. Arturo Illía became the next president in October of 1963.

In June, 1966, Argentina experienced the fourth military takeover in a period of eleven years. A group headed by General Juan Carlos Ongania forced Illía out and dissolved the national and provincial legislatures. The governors of provinces were removed and all political parties were suspended. Members of the Supreme Court were replaced, and university activities were stopped or severely limited.

Under the kind of "benevolent" dictatorship that came from this takeover, inflation has been slowed and foreign investments have been encouraged. There is a new trend toward prosperity.

The Argentine people, however, live uneasily in the knowledge that the great democracy which so many of their ancestors sought and which has been denied them throughout their history has still not come to them.

Nevertheless, the economy of the country has been very much improved by the new government under Carlos Ongania. In 1968, Argentina became a member of the International Monetary Fund. Only countries with sound money are permitted to be members of this group.

The Government of Argentina

Children of the United States might envy the children of Argentina, who have two holidays to celebrate two entirely different independence days—May 25 and July 9. The first real constitution of Argentina was adopted in 1853.

According to the constitution, the Argentine Republic is made up of twenty-two provinces, one national territory, and a Federal Capital District. There is a national Congress to which the provinces and the federal district have the right to elect representatives. This Congress has two chambers, as in the United States—a Senate and a Chamber of Deputies. There are 46 members of the Senate and 187 representatives in the Chamber. Two senators are elected from each province. One deputy is elected for each 85,000 persons in the country.

The president, vice-president, and senators hold office for six years, deputies for four. As in the United States, the president and the vice-president are chosen by electors. They may not succeed themselves, but may serve again after an interim term

has passed. All men and women over eighteen are required to vote, and are fined if they do not.

The provinces govern all matters except those over which the federal government has been given power specifically by the constitution. Each province has its own local government, with the power to make and enforce laws governing its affairs.

A five-member Supreme Court of the Nation heads the judicial system. There are five federal courts of appeal, each with three members. Each province also has its federal district court.

The constitution provides for religious freedom for all, but it also makes Argentina a Catholic nation by law. The president and the vice-president must be Roman Catholics.

In recent years, with the many changes of leaders and the strong part played by military leaders and military forces, the government of Argentina appears to be unpredictable to outside observers. The constitution seems to have been set aside.

Teaching and Learning

Even 350 years ago, bright young men in Argentina were able to go to a university in their own country. The Jesuits founded a seminary at Córdoba in 1609, and by 1613 it was a university—the fourth oldest in the Western Hemisphere. Under the Jesuits the university became great, but then declined as the years passed. Today the University of Córdoba again is one of the finest places to get a higher education— a university with a proud tradition three centuries old.

Argentina has more than 340 institutions of higher learning. Nine national universities are government supported. Government universities have no entrance examination for a high school graduate, and tuition is free. However, if a student fails a course and wants to take it again, he has to pay the fee a second time.

Probably the most widely known of the government universities is the University of Buenos Aires. It was founded in 1821 so that Argentina would have a university where science could be taught without the control of the Catholic church.

Two prominent institutions devoted to special subjects are the National Conservatory of Music and the Institute of Farm Technology.

"Education is the master key that opens the door to prosperity and makes a nation happy," José de San Martín once said. Argentina has taken these words of its liberator to heart ever since.

In 1884 a law was passed declaring education to be free and compulsory for all children between six and fourteen.

Later educational leaders of Argentina include Manuel Belgrano and Domingo

University of Buenos Aires Law School.

Domingo Faustine Sarmiento.

Faustine Sarmiento. Manuel Belgrano was called the "first great champion of public education," and Domingo Sarmiento became known as the "schoolmaster president."

There are more than 20,000 public and private elementary schools in the country and more than 5,000 high schools. Nearly three and a half million pupils attend school, being taught by over 180,000 teachers. Over 400,000 people are studying in the vocational schools of Argentina. Today Argentina leads all Latin America in the percentage of people who can read and write—ninety-one percent of the population.

Left: The University of Córdoba.
Opposite: Elementary school children in the Boca section of Buenos Aires.

47

The People of Argentina

No one knows how long men and women have lived in what is now Argentina. Cave paintings in color near Río Gallegos are reminders of ancient peoples. Other prehistoric relics are found in such places as the caves in Tierra del Fuego and the Valley of Calchaqui.

ORIGINAL INHABITANTS—THE INDIANS

Before Europeans came to the area, the tribes of the Inca rulers had pushed down into northern Argentina from Peru. The great road, Camino de los Incas, paved with stone, came from the mountains into the plains west of Tucumán. Some of the Inca roads and other signs of their extraordinary civilization still exist in Argentina. However, the Indians who had lived in the region for thousands of years stopped the invaders, and the mighty power of the Inca was halted in what is now northern Argentina. They did not extend their empire south of Tucumán.

When Europeans first came to the region, approximately ten principal Indian nations lived in what is now Argentina. The total Indian population was probably never more than half a million; today the number has dropped to a handful, totaling about 15,000 who are pure Indians.

Today some Guaraní Indians are found in the northeast. The unchanged Coya Indians of the highlands near Bolivia still live their stone-age lives, and descendants of the Quechuas also live in the northwestern highlands. Small numbers of Araucanians and Patagonians still live in western Patagonia.

Other tribes are remembered only through names of places or through history. The Patagonia, Chaco, and Pampa

These Coya Indians in the highlands near Bolivia live in the same way they did before any Europeans came to South America.

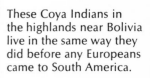

Indians were never really conquered by the Spanish, but they often fought the Araucanian Indians who came across the mountains from Chile and tried to take over the region. These Araucanian tribesmen were said to be better horsemen than the gauchos.

INDIAN CUSTOMS

The late-coming Araucanian people were skilled in many crafts. They made tents of horsehide or cowhide. Cutting the hide from the hind leg of a colt, they dried it on their feet and so created a serviceable kind of shoe. It was the Araucanian craftsmen who thought of the *boleadoras* (bola), stones on the ends of a rope, later used by the gauchos as well as lassoes.

After the Araucanian Indians, the Indians living on the slopes of the Andes were the most advanced of the early peoples. They built permanent villages, with houses made of stone walls, covered with branches, and waterproofed with thatch. Just as did the North American Indians, they grew squash, corn, and beans, and in the northerly regions, the valuable potato. These Indians were skilled in weaving cloth and baskets and also in pottery making.

The Guaraní Indians also grew crops—sweet potatoes and cassava, as well as corn and squash. They often built large group houses of logs in which many families lived. They made coarse textiles and excellent dugout canoes and were skilled fishermen.

The Querandí Indians were one of the more primitive tribes. They roasted and ground locusts, making bread from this locust flour. Lacking other means of capturing deer, they trained themselves to run after a deer for two or three days until the animal fell, exhausted.

Few picturesque tribes or Indian customs remain in Argentina today. Perhaps the most interesting modern symbol of the Indian is the round hat, like a derby, still worn by the Coya Indian women.

MAKEUP OF THE POPULATION

People of European background make up more than ninety-seven percent of the Argentine population today. Indians and part Indians, called *mestizos,* total only about two percent of the population. Negroes and those of mixed Negro and Caucasian or Indian blood make up the rest, less than one percent. Some Negroes were brought to Argentina as slaves, but were soon absorbed into the general population. Today the largest number of Negroes live in the Tucumán area.

Eighty-four percent of the Argentine people are native born, with only sixteen percent born in foreign lands. Two-thirds of all the people live in cities and towns. Roman Catholics make up ninety-four percent of the population; two percent are Protestant, and about 450,000 are members of the Jewish faith.

A gaucho on the pampa demonstrates the way a boleadoras should be swung.

For nearly three hundred years, people born in Argentina but of Spanish descent —known as *Creoles*—were the most numerous and powerful. Of course, the influence of the Spanish is still the strongest in Argentina, with people of British background probably the next most powerful.

The Italians are one of the most important ethnic groups in Argentina. Italian immigrants introduced Italian foods and other customs, and many Italian expressions have become part of the language or have changed existing words.

Patagonia has been settled extensively by people from England, Scotland, and Wales. In fact, the city of Puerto Madryn is known as "Little Wales." Even so, people of Chilean background make up forty percent of the Patagonian population.

Like New York City, Buenos Aires is known as a melting pot of nationalities, including almost all European countries. The people of the city are known as *porteños,* "people of the port." They like to think of themselves as "vivos" or "live ones."

After World War II, a great flood of displaced persons came from Europe, the largest number being Germans. Nearly twenty-two percent of the present population of Argentina is of German or central European descent. Many of these refugees were educated and highly trained. About 750,000 people are of Arab descent, mostly Lebanese Christians.

There are two German daily newspapers in Buenos Aires, and one each in Yiddish, Italian, and English.

THE GAUCHOS

Lonely, colorfully dressed, often cruel, fiercely devoted to freedom, the nomadic horsemen of the pampas made a name in history as the picturesque gauchos. In the earliest days the gaucho eked out a solitary and dangerous living hunting wild horses and cattle on the plains. As did the cowboys of North America, the gaucho became an almost legendary figure.

Quite real, however, is the contribution made by gaucho cavalry in winning Argentina's independence from Spain.

It was the gaucho who fought off the Indians and made the pampas his domain. The gauchos fought almost as hard to defend their wild land against wire fences and great orderly estancias when they first appeared. Today, the historic gaucho is gone. The modern gaucho is a colorful cowhand, working for the ranch owners. Many of today's gauchos even belong to unions.

The old gaucho lives on, however, as the most cherished historic figure of the country. His independent and battling spirit is immortalized in countless stories and songs. At hundreds of festivals and barbecues each year, people gather in gaucho costume to sing gaucho songs and dance gaucho dances. Their melodies and rhythms seem to have come from the loneliness of the pampas and the loping gait of the horses on the pampas.

Many modern cowboys continue to wear the unusual gaucho costume, with its baggy pants, called *bombachas,* short boots with

This gaucho is watching over his barbecue.

spurs, black felt sombrero, and poncho.

The old gaucho saddle was so big and fully equipped that it looked almost like a "camper" mounted on horseback. In his saddle the gaucho could carry everything he needed for weeks on the trail away from the hut he called home. His wife and children waited there for an occasional visit from their husband and father.

Few gauchos today probably know how to make the *taba* from the knucklebone of a cow. This was a favorite gambling piece for a game played something in the manner of tossing a coin. Most gaucho games were rougher. Gauchos loved horse racing and also a game in which a number of men on horseback competed for a roast duck which had been sewed into a leather bag. This was the original game of pató. In their roughest sport, two lines of gauchos sat opposite one another on horses. One gaucho would try to ride the entire distance between the lines

53

without having his horse's legs caught with a skillfully thrown bola, which would throw the gaucho to the ground.

The gauchos also liked to sit around the campfire, playing guitars and singing ballads, as the modern gauchos still do.

Lengthy gaucho duels at one time were common, with two gauchos fighting it out with their eighteen-inch knives. These fights sometimes lasted more than an hour and still occur occasionally. The gauchos seldom had gunfights.

PEOPLE OF THE STRETCHED BELT

Argentina is often called the "land of the stretched belt" because its people eat so much beef. They say their beef, fattened on pampas grass, has the best flavor in the world. The population averages at least one steak (*biftec*) a day per person. When an Argentine is not eating beefsteak, he may be enjoying lamb prepared in one of the traditional barbecues. Lamb carcasses at a barbecue are skewered on hardwood sticks that are stuck in the ground, and the lamb is roasted over a quebracho-wood fire.

Other national dishes include *puchero*, said to be one of the most delicious ways of boiling meat; *bife a caballo* (known as beef on horseback—a steak "ridden" by two fried eggs); *carbonada* (a kind of stew with meat, peaches, and thirty-six other ingredients); *puchero de gallina* (sausage,

Below left: A gaucho enjoys a gourd of mate. Below right: A gaucho on the job.

chicken, corn, potatoes, and squash all cooked together); *chorizo* (a kind of really "hot" hot dog); *empanada* (delicious meat pie); and a dessert call *dulce de leche*.

One of the most common social practices in Argentina of the past was the ritual of mate. Tea brewed from the mate leaves was served in a gourd and passed from one person to another, with everyone drinking from the same silver straw. This custom is now dying out. Buenos Aires has a legend about mate—the stranger who drinks this tea will never be able to resist returning to the city.

In northwest Argentina many people chew another kind of leaf, the coca. This dulls the senses and perhaps takes away the pain of the people who live a hard life in this region.

The Argentine national sport is soccer, brought in by the English in the 1870's. There is hardly a more colorful spectacle anywhere than the scene of a soccer game played at River Plate Stadium in Buenos Aires before 100,000 excited fans. A more unusual sport is pató (duck), a sort of basketball played on horseback with a four-handled ball.

The tango is as traditional in Argentina as soccer. This dance developed from the *habañera*, a Cuban song. It was not considered respectable until it was danced in Paris. Then members of Argentine society danced it enthusiastically. Composer-singer

Below: Argentines prepare traditional barbecued lamb.

Opposite: Pató (duck) is played, a game that originated from the gaucho game in which men competed for a roast duck which had been sewed into a leather bag.

PANAGRA

Right: Schoolboys in Palermo Park, Buenos Aires, play soccer, the national sport of Argentina.

BRANIFF INTERNATIONAL

Carlos Gardel developed the tango to a high point. Probably the favorite country dance of Argentina is the *gato,* generally performed by two couples.

The most typical song of the pampas is the *estilo,* describing life on the plains.

SOCIAL PROGRESS

Argentina was one of the first countries in Latin America to develop social insurance, trade unions, cooperatives, public housing, and other activities for the welfare of the people. The Ministry of Social Welfare and Public Health provides free medical care for the needy and a wide variety of other health services.

The first laborers to organize in Argentina were the railroad workers; their *La Fraternidad* was founded in 1885. Soon other labor unions had formed. Before long many of them set up low-cost housing projects for their members, built hospitals,

operated medical services and banks, and provided pensions. Today more than eight million workers are members of unions.

Workmen's compensation, old age insurance, health and accident insurance, maternity insurance, and survivors insurance are all provided. In addition there is a national pension program.

Perhaps the worst problem facing Argentina is housing. So many people need new homes that if house building doubled it would take twenty years to provide enough homes. Although there are few really poor people in Buenos Aires, the city has thirty-three slum districts. People who could well afford to live in better homes simply have nowhere to go.

Another major problem of the people is inflation. For many years the cost of living rose so rapidly that many people were forced to work at two or even three jobs just to provide for their needs. Recently the cost of living has risen less rapidly.

57

Human Treasures

EL LIBERTADOR—SAN MARTÍN

One of the greatest military feats in all human history was performed by a native of Argentina. Because of this and his many other achievements, he became a hero of independence. He was José de San Martín, hailed by the people of Argentina as El Libertador—the liberator.

Born on February 25, 1778, in the village of Yapeyú, San Martín was sent to Spain in 1785, where he studied at the Seminary of the Nobles in Madrid. At thirteen he entered the Spanish army, and at that young age fought well in the battle of Oran against the Moors.

For more than twenty years San Martín fought for Spain. He might have become wealthy and successful in the service of the king. Hearing that his native land might become independent, however, he joined the independence movement. In 1811 he left Spain secretly for London, where he met leaders of the independence movement.

Coming to Argentina in 1812, he had many successes before the greatest success of all—crossing the Andes and capturing Chile. For this and his later victories he has been called one of the most brilliant generals in military history. Most people consider San Martín's crossing of the Andes more difficult and more successful than the crossing of the Alps by Hannibal or Napoleon.

After much preparation, San Martín also led an expedition to the Spanish stronghold of Peru. The Spanish fled and the people received San Martín with great enthusiasm, naming him the "Protector" of Peru.

On July 26, 1822, the two greatest South American leaders—Simón Bolívar and José de San Martín—met at Guayaquil, Ecuador. Bolívar exclaimed, "At last my wishes of meeting and shaking the hand of the renowned General San Martín have been fulfilled."

At a banquet Bolívar boastfully proposed a toast: "To the two greatest men in South America—General San Martín and myself." San Martín responded more modestly: "To the early end of the war, to the organization of the various republics of the continent, and to the health of the Liberator of Colombia."

San Martín offered to serve under Bolívar so that the continent might be completely freed from Spain. However, for his own private reasons Bolívar refused to accept.

As soon as Peru seemed ready to govern itself, San Martín prepared to withdraw. He wrote in a letter: " . . . I am tired of being called tyrant and of having it said that I wish to become king. . . . As my youth was sacrificed in the service of Spain and my middle age in the service of my native land, I believe that I have the right to dispose of my old age."

In his farewell address to the people of Peru, San Martín said: "I have witnessed the declaration of independence of the states of Chile and Peru. I hold in my hands the standard which Pizarro brought to enslave the empires of the Incas; and I have ceased to be a public man. My

General José de San Martín.

promise to the countries for which I fought is fulfilled—to secure their independence and leave them to select their own governments. The presence of a fortunate soldier, however disinterested he may be, is dangerous to newly established states."

After the death of his wife in Buenos Aires, San Martín took his little daughter María Mercedes to Europe, where he lived the rest of his life as a poor man in lonely exile, blind for the last few years before his death. When he died at Boulogne-sur-Mer in France on August 17, 1850, only seven persons attended his funeral.

Only after his death did Argentina recognize José de San Martín as the national hero. At last his body was returned with ceremonies and honor to his homeland and now lies revered in the cathedral at Buenos Aires. Countless monuments have been erected in his honor throughout South America.

"The cause I defend is the cause of humankind," San Martín once wrote. Later he said: "I desired to sacrifice everything to promote the liberty of my native land." Few other leaders have made so many sacrifices or have been so unselfish in any cause.

His "noble generosity" made him a most remarkable man. In Mendoza he gave half his salary as governor toward training and equipping the army. When the city of Santiago, Chile, gave him a gift of 10,000 pesos, he gave the money to establish a library. He donated income from a farm in Chile to health work in the country. San Martín refused to accept the position of ruler in Chile and gave up the leadership of Peru as soon as he was no longer needed there.

The Pan American Union has stated: "History has pronounced him a military genius, whose moral courage, humanitarianism, and selfless devotion to great ideals set him apart for all time."

OTHER PUBLIC FIGURES

Other heroes of Argentine independence were Mariano Moreno, Manuel Belgrano, and Martín Guëmes.

Mariano Moreno has been called the "soul of the revolution of 1810." He served as the secretary of the first junta that ruled the newly independent country. His ideas were so democratic that his more conservative fellow associates could not accept many of them. He is also remembered as the founder of Argentina's national library.

Among his many other patriotic activities, General Belgrano created the national flag of Argentina.

General Guëmes was one of Argentina's greatest military leaders, noted for his generalship of the gauchos, who fought fiercely in their baggy scarlet uniforms.

Domingo F. Sarmiento, called both Argentina's greatest president and its greatest writer, also served as minister to the United States. Another well-loved president was Hipólito Irigoyen.

One of the country's great historians was Bartolomé Mitre, who wrote a biography of San Martín. He also founded the Buenos Aires newspaper, *La Nación*.

Left: Bartolomé Mitre, historian. Above: Mariano Moreno, liberal leader and hero of Argentine independence.

CREATIVE ARGENTINES

In Argentine literature two writings are generally considered masterworks— *Facundo* by Domingo Sarmiento and *Martín Fierro* by José Hernández. Both works tell about the fascinating life of the gaucho. The long six-thousand-line poem by Hernandez, according to one critic, is "a primitive poem written by an educated man. . . . It can be read on various levels: as an entertaining story, as a protest against social injustice and a record of historical conditions. . . . " The poem is loved greatly by Argentines of all types and is thought of as the national poem.

Argentina's first novelist was José Marmol. Also a poet, he boasted that his first verses were scribbled on the walls of the cell where the dictator Rosas had imprisoned him. Another prominent writer of fiction was Manuel Gálvez. Miguel Cané was known for his recollections of school days, which he called *Juvenilia*.

Esteban Echeverría was a social reformer and a poet. He established the group of writers known as the Generation of 1837. Poet Horacio Quiroga became known as the Poet of the Río de la Plata. His writing vividly described the horrors of Chaco jungles.

The greatest playwright of Argentina was Florencio Sánchez, who wrote three major plays, *La gringa*, *M'hijo el doctor*, and *Barranca Abajo*.

Modern-day writers of Argentina include the Argentine writer who produced the greatest volume of work—Leopoldo Lugones. Others are novelist Enrique Rodriquez Larreta; historian Ricardo Rojas; Enrique Banchs, considered by many to be the country's greatest living poet; two writers of gaucho stories, Benito Lynch and Ricardo Güiraldes; Jorge Luis Borges, poet and prose writer; and Eduardo Mallea, one of the foremost writers of today.

Life on the pampas and the customs of the gaucho were preserved on canvas by painter Prilidiano Pueyrredón.

Argentine art ranks among the most highly developed in the hemisphere. The country has ninety-eight art museums in both large and small towns.

Much of the music and dance of Argentina comes from the songs, dances, and primitive musical instruments of the Indians. Spaniards also brought their own music and instruments. The most typical song of the pampas is the *estilo*, dealing with life on the plains.

Argentina has many modern composers. Juan José Castro is internationally known for his operas and symphonies, and Juan Carlos Paz is a leading modern composer. Ginasterra composed *Bomarzo*, a modern opera. The world premiere was held in Lincoln Center, New York, in 1968.

The National Museum of Art in Buenos Aires, one of the many museums in Argentina.

VARIG AIRLINES

62

Natural Treasures

LIVING TREASURES

The hard riding gaucho bears down on the "critter." He throws his bola—a kind of lasso with heavy balls at each end that wrap around the legs of the creature it is thrown at. The gaucho's aim is good, and the creature falls. Instead of a bellowing calf or cow, however, one sees a flutter of wings and a flurry of feathers.

The scene is a roundup of rheas, huge birds somewhat like the African ostrich. Captured for their feathers, which are used for dusters and other household purposes, the rheas are released later to grow more feathers for the next roundup.

Rheas are the largest and perhaps the most interesting of Argentina's vast number of birds. If one is lucky, he might sometimes see a parade of eight or ten baby rheas being shepherded by their father.

Another bird which struts around in an awkward upright walk was the wonder of the Cavendish expedition at Puerto Deseado in 1586. The explorers gave the bird the name meaning "white head"—*pengwyn*. These lovable, gawky birds have been called penguins ever since.

One of the world's most stately birds is the majestic condor, soaring silently above the lofty Andes. Completely different, but also fascinating, is the cataract swift that darts behind Iguazú Falls to catch its food.

The national bird of Argentina is the hornero, or oven bird. It makes an oven-like nest of straw coated with mud, with a curving entrance like a tunnel to keep out the rain. Nearly every pampas telephone pole has one of these nests with the owner sitting rather pompously outside.

The bird life of the pampas is one of the most interesting features of the region.

The national bird of Argentina, the hornero, or oven bird, makes a round nest with a tunnel-like entrance.

Flights of flamingos often look like large pink clouds. Heron egrets and the distinguished pink spoonbills are numerous.

In the Chaco are hordes of storks, swans, and waterfowl of many kinds, as well as less numerous eagles and vultures.

Swans, geese, and ducks are seen throughout the year in large numbers in the lake region. The island of Tierra del Fuego alone has 152 species of birds—one of the noblest being the Antarctic wild goose.

Argentina is a game bird hunter's paradise, especially for doves, duck, and partridge. A hunter of the perdiz partridge would not be surprised to bring in a hundred of these delicious-tasting game birds in a single day.

North Americans come to Argentina in large numbers to shoot the impressive red stag, long hunted only by royalty in Europe. A few lucky hunters may witness the stags snorting, pawing, and clashing in head-rattling fury as they fight for a mate.

The fat hares of Patagonia are killed by the thousands, but they continue to multiply so fast they are considered almost a national plague.

The wild members of the cat family in Argentina are the lynx, jaguar, puma, and the endearing ocelot, known as the "horseman of the trees." Sleeping in the trees by day, he hunts at night. Ocelots are favorite pets of many Argentines.

In the higher regions of the country llamas, alpacas, vicuñas, and miniature donkeys leap from crag to crag with all the grace of ballet dancers. The vicuña is tremendously valued for its unbelievably soft and beautiful fur. The vicuña are so prized that they have been hunted until they are almost extinct.

Some fishermen consider the pejerrey fish one of the prize catches to be found anywhere. It is a kind of combination of salmon, trout, sunfish, and sole. Another much prized fish is the dorado of the Paraná River.

GROWING TREASURES

Large areas of northern and southern Argentina are covered with forests of valuable trees. When first discovered, the pampas were almost without trees. Solitary ombu trees stood out like sentinels for miles across the plains. Millions of trees have been planted in recent years, including the favorite jacarandá trees that line mile after mile of streets in Buenos Aires. These bloom in a spectacular showing of beauty in the December summer.

One of the most valuable trees is the quebracho, as hard as iron, that grows in great forests in the Chaco.

Among the strangest of trees is the palo barracho. Its thorny trunk grows at a tipsy angle; its seedpods, shaped like bottles, ripen and open to show dark brown seeds cradled in cream-colored cotton, which is used for stuffing in mattresses and cushions.

A red flower with an unusual pulpy bud is Argentina's national flower, named the ceibo.

MINERALS

Although iron and steel have been scarce in Argentina, a reserve of 900,000,000 tons of iron ore has been found in the Sierra Grande.

The first petroleum was discovered in Argentina in 1907. Since that time, much oil has been found. The present reserves of petroleum in Argentina are estimated at 3,700,000,000 barrels. Natural gas reserves are found to equal 1,411,000,000 barrels of petroleum.

Jacarandá trees line the streets of the Avenue Nueve de Julio in Buenos Aires.

The People Use Their Treasures

AGRICULTURE

More of Argentina's wealth comes from agriculture than from any other source. Value of farm products of the country totals about two billion dollars per year. Crops bring in a little more than half of this total and livestock a little less than half. Only about a tenth of all the land in Argentina is used for farming.

During the early years, stock raising was the only industry. Herding the rangy stringy cattle, the picturesque gauchos roamed the pampas. The great number of cattle were descended from those left by the earliest Spanish explorers. Tough dried beef (*tasajo*) and hides were the earliest products sold.

Later, refrigerated ships were able to carry Argentine beef to Europe. However, Europeans did not like the leathery meat of the wiry range cattle, so estancia owners hurried to improve the quality of their herds, importing prize cattle from across the sea. They also found that their herds would grow fat and tender eating the alfalfa that thrived in Argentina. The first estancia was fenced in 1854, making possible the modern cattle industry. Today there are more than forty-five million head of beef cattle in Argentina.

European farmers were encouraged to come to Argentina; many were given free use of a farm. They could grow wheat or other crops for three years. The fourth year the farmers had to plant the land in alfalfa and move on. The owner of the land could then count on the alfalfa growing and feeding his cattle for as long as ten years.

Eventually many landowners found that they could make as much money from growing wheat as they could from cattle.

Magnificent Argentine cattle grazing in good pasture.

Today wheat is the largest single crop of Argentina, with a value of $261,000,000 in 1966. However, beef is still king of agriculture, bringing in $604,800,000 in 1966 alone.

Corn is the third most important farm income source—$211,200,000; then grapes, $165,400,000; milk, $150,100,000; and wool, $115,000,000. Other important farm income producers are sugarcane, potatoes, mutton, pork, cotton fiber, and flaxseed.

Sheep raising is the most important industry of vast Patagonia, where there are two and a half sheep for every person. The fifty million sheep of Argentina total more than twice the human population, and the country ranks fourth in the world in wool production.

The great estancias are still important in Argentina, with some of the ranches

67

Opposite: House on an estancia with the ever-present windmill in the background. BRANIFF INTERNATIONAL
Above: There are more than twice as many sheep in Argentina as there are people.
Here they are grazing on a rocky slope. ALPHA

covering as much as ten square miles. Windmills stand like sentinels in the fields. From the windmills radiate long metal troughs from which the livestock drink. The pastures (*potreros*) are large, covering from a hundred to five thousand acres. These are surrounded by heavy, expensive wire fences, held up by iron-hard quebracho posts. Sheep, horses, and cattle all graze in the same field.

Most estancias have rather large houses, smaller office buildings for running the ranch, and a few sheds for sheltering ewes and lambs. There may be some small houses for the peons who work on the farm, and in some of the larger pastures are huts for the peons who take care of the fences and animals in those pastures.

One of the important advances in farming in recent years is irrigation. More than

Left: Sugarcane is being loaded for the cane mills at Tucamán, the center of sugar production in Argentina. Below: Avenida General Paz, one small section of Argentina's forty thousand miles of highways.

Railroads have contributed more than anything else to the development of Argentina. Many of them have been built over mountains, as was this line at Mendoza.

a million acres of land are irrigated in the area of Tucumán alone. The Río Negro valley now has irrigated fruit orchards, and new irrigation projects are constantly being put into operation in other parts of the country.

Leather goods and furs are important export items. Furs include the costly vicuña, skunk, puma, nutria, and spotted jaguar.

TRANSPORTATION

Railroads have contributed more than anything else to the development of Argentina. In 1857 the first six miles of railroad track were built, running southwest from Buenos Aires. A wide-gauge locomotive used by the British in the Crimean War was imported to run on this track, a first modern use of "war surplus." The railroad between Rosario and Córdoba was completed in 1870, the first major railroad in Argentina.

By 1890, nearly six thousand miles of railroad track had been laid, and by 1908 the railroad had reached the Bolivian border. One of the world's "superhuman" engineering feats, laying the railroad over the towering Andes, was accomplished in 1910. Even more amazing was the Huaytiquina railway, running from Salta to Antofagasta, Chile. This track snakes its way over a 14,680-foot mountain pass.

Almost forty percent of the railroad mileage of all South America is found in Argentina—27,284 miles.

Before railroads, freight was moved across country in huge lumbering oxcarts weighing as much as two tons. There were no roads or highways for these carts and they had to make their way over rutted trails, sometimes sinking deep into the earth. Covered wagons, like those used in the United States, were known as *carretas* on the frontiers of Argentina.

Highways have been built slowly in Argentina. One of the greatest periods of highway building began in 1932 with more than thirty thousand miles of highways built in ten years. Another great push in highway building came during the presidency of Arturo Frondizi. Four sections of the Pan American Highway branch out from Buenos Aires. One section of the Pan American Highway follows almost exactly the historic road laid down by the ancient Inca highway engineers, crossing the Andes over towering Uspallata Pass. This portion of the highway is known as the San Martín sector, in honor of the hero who urged his army along much the same route.

Highways in Argentina total about forty thousand miles. After the United States, Argentina has the most extensive network of transportation in the Western Hemisphere.

Buenos Aires is one of the world's great seaports. Keeping the port open, however, is a constant fight with the Paraná and other rivers, since they pile mud into the bay. Only constant dredging of the Río de la Plata keeps the port of Buenos Aires open.

About two thousand miles of rivers and waterways carry freight and passenger boats and barges in Argentina. Some of the world's great river navigation systems come together at the Río de la Plata. These are the Paraná, Uruguay, Paraguay, and Alta Paraná rivers. The traffic that travels on these rivers is vital not only to Argentina but also to Brazil, Uruguay, and Paraguay. Riverboats chug up the mile-wide island-dotted Río Negro as far as Nequén.

When Ezeiza International Airport was built by President Juan Perón it seemed to be an unusable white elephant. Today it ranks with the great airports of the world, and is still one of the largest. Argentina's most important airline is Aerolíneas Argentinas, owned by the nation. It has a large number of flights throughout Argentina and into the rest of South America, as well as to North America and Europe.

COMMUNICATION

Argentina has some of the world's finest newspapers. Two of the best-known and most highly respected newspapers anywhere are *La Prensa* and *La Nación*. The Buenos Aires *Herald* is considered one of the finest English-language newspapers published outside of an English-speaking country.

Buenos Aires has had as many as twelve daily newspapers published at one time. The city is ranked as one of the great publishing centers of the world, with over a hundred publishing houses.

The people of Argentina saw their first television in 1951. Today, there are a number of television stations, but only 1,600,-000 Argentines had television sets in 1965, compared with more than 70,000,-000 in the United States. In the same year, Argentina had 6,200,000 radios.

INDUSTRY

The first large-scale industry of Argentina was that of the *saladero*—plants where meat and hides were salted to preserve them for export. Beginning about 1810, this industry was the basis for many large Argentine fortunes, including that of dictator de Rosas.

Industry did not begin to grow in Argentina until about 1880. Progress was hindered by the lack of coal, electrical power, iron ore, and other metals. Imports of fuel and machinery came from Britain.

More workers make a living in the food industry than in any other. Today Argentina processes almost all the foodstuffs needed within the country. Manufacturing of consumer goods increased so rapidly that by 1955 local industry produced ninety-nine percent of all that was required. This is true in spite of the fact that Argentina still does not have enough of the backbones of industry—electric power and steel.

The steel industry is growing, however. The large steel complex at San Nicholas is what is known as a "completely integrated" steel plant. Here there are coke ovens, a blast furnace, open hearths, a by-products plant, and mills to produce rails, rolled plates and sheets, and tinplate.

The automobile industry is one of the fastest growing. In the period 1958 through

The automobile industry thrives in Argentina.
Above: The Fiat plant at Córdoba.
Left: The Kaiser plant.

1960 more than twenty auto manufacturers began to assemble their cars in Argentina, using imported parts. Only a few years later ninety-five percent of all Argentine cars were made locally.

There are over 3,500 textile plants in Argentina which include nylon and rayon in their production. One of the world's most complete cotton processing plants operates at Resistencia. Argentina's foot-wear industry is one of the most highly developed in Latin America.

At least eighty percent of the world supply of quebracho extract (tannin) comes from the red quebracho of Argentina. This is used in the tanning of leather. The white quebracho tree supplies timber for railroad ties and fence posts.

Buenos Aires is the largest manufacturing center. Mendoza is noted for its large wineries; Rosario for steel mills and metal factories, oil refineries, tractors, meat packing, chemicals, and tanning; Córdoba is the automotive center; Santa Fe is known for zinc and copper smelting, flour mills, and dairy products; Tucumán for sugar refineries; and the Chaco region for cotton gins and sawmills.

The first modern oil refinery in Argentina was built in La Plata in 1925. By 1962 Argentina was producing and refining enough petroleum and natural gas to meet all its needs. Petroleum is produced or refined at Comodoro Rivadavia, Santa Cruz, Salta, Tierra del Fuego, Chubut, Mendoza, and Bahía Blanca.

Only a limited supply of coal is mined in Patagonia, Mendoza, and San Juan.

Argentina produced only 5,320,000 kilowatts of electricity in 1965, compared to 8,500,000 for Switzerland. New electric plants are being opened at an increasing rate, however.

TRADE AND BANKING

"World's largest exporter of beef" is one of Argentina's proudest titles. The country ranks fifteenth among all the leading trading countries of the world.

Goods worth $1,593,000,000 were exported by Argentina in 1966, while the country imported only $1,124,000,000 worth. Because it sold more goods than it bought, Argentina had a favorable balance of trade. In 1966 this amounted to $469,000,000.

The nation's main exports are wheat and corn (twenty-eight percent), meat and meat products (twenty-three percent), and wool (nine percent). By far the most costly imports are machinery and vehicles of all kinds, which had a value of $728,000,000 in 1966.

The Central Bank of Argentina is the government bank. It administers the banking law, regulates the amount of credit and the interest rate.

Sheet metal ready to be poured in a steel mill in Buenos Aires.

SIDERUGIA ARGENTINA

The Enchantment of Argentina

"GLORY OF THE GLOBE"

"Dazzling, sophisticated, the Paris of South America, glittering, brilliant"—almost all the words of praise in the dictionary have been used by lovers of Buenos Aires to describe their favorite city. There is little doubt that the city is one of the greatest on the globe—ninth largest metropolis in the world—larger than Madrid, Paris, Rome, or Berlin.

Argentina's capitol building (Palacio del Congreso Nacional) towers over one of the most beautiful and unusual cities to be found anywhere. The great domed building was designed along the lines of the Capitol of the United States. Inside, the corridors and galleries gleam with the elegance of gold and marble. The majestic white marble building faces the monument and fountains of Plaza del Congreso. Tearing down four city blocks, the builders of this plaza built and landscaped it in only eighty days to have it ready for Argentina's one-hundredth anniversary celebration. Nearby are the National Lottery Building and the monumental National Postal Savings Bank.

The president's house takes its name from its color, as does the White House in the United States. This is the *Casa Rosada,* or "Pink House." The story is told that President Domingo F. Sarmiento wanted to please both political parties of his time. One party wore red badges, the other white badges. When it came time to redecorate the president's house, Sarmiento had the two colors mixed. The result was pink, and the mansion has been pink ever since.

The Pink House stands on the Plaza de Mayo, still called the "heart of the city," as it was in the early days. A neighbor of the Pink House is the historic old Cabildo, or city hall, from which Buenos Aires was

Above: The Casa Rosada (the pink house) on the Plaza de Mayo, is where the president lives. Left: The entrance to the Casa Rosada.

governed in past times. In the plaza also are the municipal building and the great Cathedral of Buenos Aires. In a mausoleum of the cathedral lie the bones of the liberator, José de San Martín. An eternal flame burns in constant tribute to the hero. San Martín is also honored in another of the great plazas of the city—the Plaza San Martín. The city has reproduced the house where San Martín died in Boulogne-sur-Mer, France. Here many mementos of his life are on display.

There are not very many old buildings or old sections of the city. The oldest *barrio* (district) of the city is San Telmo. Here one of the popular old buildings, the

Casa de los Santos Ejercicios, is used as a convent. The oldest colonial building of the city is the Church of San Ignacio de Loyola, built in 1710. The American Church, established in 1863, was the first of its kind in Latin America.

Avenida Nueve de Julio, 450 feet wide, is the widest street in the world. Taking its name from the day Argentina declared independence in 1816, the street is a glittering combination of tree-shaded central mall, bustling traffic, and imposing buildings of every type.

Calle Florida is the city's busiest shopping street, said by its admirers to have some of the finest shops in the world. One of these is acclaimed as the largest drug-store anywhere. This is Farmacia Franco Inglesa, where the clerks speak almost every language known.

Another "record-holding" street is Rivadavia Street, often considered the longest in the world.

A contrast to the modern avenues is quaint El Caminito, named for a famous tango. The colorful little street has been restored by Benito Quinquela Martin. Now it is an open-air museum by day and a theater by night. The people who live in the brightly painted houses often take part in the plays.

Under the streets of Buenos Aires are the famous subways—five complete systems. The people are especially proud of the beautiful subway stations lining the routes. The city opened its first *subterráneo* in 1911. Since then the system has been expanding, but not fast enough to keep up with the crushing crowds that pile on at rush hour. Visitors are delighted to find that they can ride anywhere on the five interconnecting systems for ten pesos, about three cents.

Buenos Aires is also known for its 150 spacious parks, with the beautiful Palermo Park the largest and most famous of all. Its famous rose gardens, ponds dotted with waterfowl, Spanish tiled patios, waterways, and winding paths are crowded every weekend. Nearby are the botanical gardens and the large zoo.

A trip to the airport near the southern suburb of Ezeiza brings into view one of the hemisphere's greatest air terminals. Its swimming pools, hotel, restaurants, and other attractions make it more like an ultramodern resort than a travel terminal. Less than thirty miles from the heart of Buenos Aires, Ezeiza International Airport is reached by a new express highway.

Another special attraction of Buenos Aires is the National Cattle Show, one of the world's finest. Every year toward the end of July the work of *estancieros* in breeding pedigreed herds is demonstrated to livestock experts from all over the world. Because cattle are so very important in the

Crowded Calle Florida, the busiest shopping street in Buenos Aires.

country, the prices paid at auction indicate whether or not Argentina will have a prosperous year.

One of the strangest sights of Buenos Aires is Recoleta Cemetery, where the burial vaults of the Argentine patricians are lined up like houses in a street. These vaults represent nearly every style of architecture.

"A MOST CULTURED CITY"

Buenos Aires is very much like a large European city. With more theaters than New York or London, seven hundred art galleries (forty-five more than Paris), the best-dressed women outside of Paris and Rome, the city has long been renowned for its culture.

Perhaps the proudest symbol of culture is the huge Teatro Colón, the opera house, seating three thousand, with room for six hundred performers on the stage.

Teatro Colón has its own opera company, symphony orchestra, ballet and musical comedy companies, handsome gold and scarlet lounges, a Museum of Lyric Art, restaurants, and banquet halls. The performances, held in one of the most beautiful opera houses in the world, are among the best held anywhere.

Teatro San Martín is an eleven-story building that houses three theaters.

Another international center of culture is the National Museum of Fine Arts, which exhibits a nearly complete collection of Argentine painters and sculptors. At the Museum of Decorative Arts there is an important collection of tapestries and antiques. The Museum of Spanish art specializes in relics of Spanish culture, such as the silver work used by gauchos on their stirrups and saddles, and the silver straws and antique mate cups from which mate tea was sipped.

Other aspects of Argentine history can be studied at the Museum of Natural History in Buenos Aires and at the Natural History Museum of the University of La Plata, in a suburb of the city.

QUEEN OF THE RIVER OF SILVER

After its permanent settlement in 1580, Buenos Aires slumbered, a drowsing village, for over two hundred years. Not until 1776 did the Spanish realize what they had been missing by keeping Buenos Aires out of the world's commerce. To the people of Buenos Aires, *porteños* (people of the port), their city is still the most important place in the hemisphere.

Probably no other city anywhere dominates its country as much as Buenos Aires does Argentina. Over thirty percent of the entire Argentine population lives in Buenos Aires, Queen of the River of Silver. The city is a magnet, drawing people from the countryside much as New York City does in the United States, but to an even greater extent.

Children play in the colorful Boca section of Buenos Aires. Paintings and sculpture are displayed in the open air throughout this artists' area.

The people of the provinces have always felt that there is fame and fortune as well as fun and excitement in Buenos Aires, and they have continued to flock to the city in great numbers—the wealthy and socially prominent as well as the poor.

There are still *villas miserias* or slum dwelling areas. However, many of the people who live there are not poor; they simply cannot get good housing because it cannot be built fast enough to meet the needs of all. Buenos Aires does not have a large population of the very poor or of the extremely rich. Most of the people of Buenos Aires make a comfortable living, and many are wealthy.

The comfortable life of the city is shown by the fact that its people eat an average of two hundred pounds of beef a year. This is twice as much as is consumed in the United States. A steak dinner may cost as little as $1.50 at a good restaurant.

Buenos Aires claims some of the world's best restaurants, with one or more in almost every block. They indicate how fond the people are of eating. Some of the most popular spots in Buenos Aires are the charming sidewalk cafés, where it is said that if you wait long enough all Buenos Aires will pass by your table.

Buenos Aires boasts half of all the telephones in South America and a large percentage of the autos in Argentina.

As the second largest metropolitan area in the hemisphere and the largest Spanish city in the world, few would quarrel with those who call Buenos Aires one of the greatest metropolitan areas.

Ringing Buenos Aires are many elegant suburbs, with fine mansions and sparkling swimming pools. A continuous line of suburbs stretches from the popular holiday resort of Tigre at the delta of the Paraná River, where it meets the Río de la Plata to Vicente-Lopez-Florida. La Plata, thirty-five miles from Buenos Aires, was a planned city, built to be the capital of Buenos Aires Province. The University of La Plata is one of the nation's outstanding universities.

OTHER IMPORTANT CITIES

Rosario The second largest city of Argentina today is Rosario, on the west bank of the Paraná River about two hundred miles north of Buenos Aires. The city is also the second most important port in the country.

Grain and other agricultural products are shipped from here and the commerce of the region is distributed by way of the many highways and railroad lines that meet here. The city is also the center of the industry of its district.

Modern and well planned, Rosario has many attractive parks and impressive boulevards. Some streets are wider than those in Buenos Aires.

Most visitors comment on the two figures of bronze atop the Minotti building—one a stalk of corn, the other of wheat—symbols of the rich farmlands surrounding Rosario.

One of the principal universities of Argentina, the University of the Litoral, has its headquarters at Rosario. Several of the

Palermo Park with its rose gardens, ponds, and winding paths, is the largest and one of the most beautiful of the parks in Buenos Aires.

The busy Port of Buenos Aires, one of the great seaports of the world.

main municipal buildings of the city are found near the river, grouped around the Plaza 25 de Mayo.

Córdoba For almost three centuries Córdoba, founded in 1573, was the most important city in Argentina. It was a leading center of education, art, and religion, and far ahead of the drowsy town of Buenos Aires. Its Universidad Mayor de San Carlos, dating from 1613, was one of the first universities in the hemisphere.

The city is famous for its early architecture. Much of the colonial section, centering around the Plaza San Martín, is well preserved. The graceful doorways, gardens and patios, carved balconies of wood, and wrought-iron grilles are reminders of old Spain.

Facing the plaza are the Cathedral, the Cabildo, and the Obispo Chapel, constructed in 1573. Among other landmarks are the viceroy's house, built in 1700, now a museum, and the colonial mansion of the Allende family.

Córdoba has many interesting churches, several of unusual architecture. Many have richly decorated interiors with wood carvings covered in gold. Most of the interiors were decorated by Guaraní Indian craftsmen under the direction of Jesuits. Among the notable churches are the Jesuit Church of la Compañia and the Church of Santo Domingo, with its beautiful Altar of the Virgin, dating from 1592. During the Fiesta of the Virgin in October, Santo Domingo displays a rare collection of church jewels.

A graceful wrought-iron portico in Córdoba.

Córdoba even today is the third largest city of the republic. It is a center for Argentina's all-year vacationland. The climate, resort hotels, and scenery draw people from all over the world.

An Academy of Fine Arts, a noted annual exhibition of art, the Museum of Fine Arts, an excellent zoo and aquarium, and

82

the astronomical observatory help Córdoba to continue its reputation as a cultural center. The observatory has much the same reputation in Argentina that the Greenwich Observatory has in England.

A folklore festival at Córdoba in January is one of the finest affairs of its type on the continent. Singing and dancing groups from all over the country compete for prizes at this festival.

Mendoza Argentina's western metropolis, Mendoza, is noted for its extraordinary beauty and for its many associations with the national hero, San Martín. From the peak of Cerro de la Gloria, overlooking the city, looms a striking monument to San Martín and his Army of the Andes. This monument is a part of San Martín Park near Mendoza.

The San Martín Museum occupies a former school building on Avenue General San Martín. Another museum is the fine Museum of Natural History, noted for its collection of Argentine animals and plants.

Much of the beauty of Mendoza lies in its wide treelined streets, many plazas, and colorful flower gardens.

Mendoza is the center for an area noted for its mountain sports. Another attraction

The Cathedral of Córdoba, facing the plaza, is one of the landmarks of the city.

of Mendoza is its *Fiesta de la Vendimia,* or Bacchus Festival of The Vineyards, held each March, which has gained worldwide fame. It features spectacular processions among other events. Much of Argentina's best wine pours from the wineries of Mendoza, and the grapes of the province are considered among the world's finest.

Tucumán   Tucumán, with more than 200,-000 people, is the biggest and most bustling city of northern Argentina. Often Tucumán is called the "Capital of the North." It also is called the "Philadelphia of Argentina," because Argentine independence was proclaimed there on July 9, 1816.

These plump, ripe grapes in Mendoza may be on their way to one of the city's famous wineries.

PANAGRA

Casa Historica, where the declaration was signed, has been restored. Plaza Belgrano, site of the important Battle of 1812, has a statue of General Belgrano, the victor in that battle.

Tucumán is also known for its many colonial buildings, the Government Palace being one of the most curious. Nearby is San Francisco Church. Another place of interest is the University of Tucumán.

In Bishop Colombres' house is the first sugar press made by the Bishop, who introduced sugarcane to the area. Today the huge sugar refineries are one of the city's main tourist attractions. The great irrigated cane fields of the region make it known as the "Garden of the Republic." A traditional sugarcane festival is held at Tucumán each year.

Resistencia and Corrientes   The charming cities of Resistencia and Corrientes lie on opposite sides of the Paraná River, just below where this mighty river is formed by the junction of the Paraguay and Alto Paraná rivers. Resistencia, capital of Chaco Province, is five miles inland, with Barrenqueras as its river port. One of the most complete cotton processing plants in the world is found at Resistencia.

Corrientes, capital of the province of the same name, is important both historically and commercially. At the Church of the Cross (La Cruz) is kept the famous cross contributed by the founder of the city, Alonzo de Vera. It is said that Indians who tried to destroy the cross were killed by a bolt of lightning from a cloudless sky.

84

This balcony in Salta is an example of the fine colonial architecture in one of Argentina's loveliest colonial cities.

Mar del Plata Mar del Plata, called "the Pearl of the Atlantic," is queen of Argentine beach resorts and one of the largest and best-known seaside centers in the world. Its casino is said to be the largest in the world and can accommodate 20,000 people. One room is 450 feet long. The permanent population of Mar del Plata is over 250,000 but it may entertain almost 2,000,000 people in a season. Among these are many wealthy aristocrats.

OTHER PLACES OF INTEREST

Some travelers call Salta Argentina's loveliest colonial city. People who build new buildings in the old style pay no taxes for several years. Among the fine colonial buildings of Salta are the churches of the seventeenth and eighteenth centuries.

There is a legend that a terrible earthquake at Salta was stopped when statues of Christ and the Virgin Mary were paraded in the town streets. Salta still celebrates the festival of the Virgin Mary, when statues are again paraded. The city is also noted for its Mardi Gras.

Another well-known festival is the Wheat Harvest Fiesta at Santa Fe in January. That city was also noted for an earthquake. The tremors of 1944 very nearly destroyed San Juan, capital of San Juan Province.

Lujan is also known for its statue of the Virgin Mary. This image was carried about the country on an oxcart. The story is told that the oxcart stuck in the mud and could not be moved. This was considered as a sign that the image should remain there. A small chapel was built and the town of Lujan grew up around it. The statue is now housed in a great basilica and people from all over the country come there on pilgrimages. May 21 is the special day of the Virgin at Lujan.

Lujan also has a colonial and historical museum. The museum Gauchesco Ricardo Guiraldes near San Antonio de Areco displays an estancia like those of the last century. The colonial church of Candonga is now a national monument.

Perhaps the most interesting relics of all are those of San Ignacio Mini. This once flourishing Jesuit mission among the Guaraní Indians had been overgrown by jungle and was not rediscovered until 1897. Here still stand the ruins of the thirty blocks of houses with masonry walls three feet thick, a large church, several public buildings, a school, and cloisters. As a memorial to the amazing Jesuits and their jungle civilization, the Argentine government has designated the area a national monument in order to preserve and restore the ruins.

What is perhaps the most famous monument in Argentina stands at a height of 12,650 feet. This is the statue of Christ the Redeemer, known as the Christ of the Andes. It marks the frontier between Argentina and Chile. The stately figure was contributed by the union workers of Argentina in the hope that "These mountains will crumble before the peoples of Argentina and Chile will break the peace sworn at the feet of Christ the Redeemer," as inscribed on the pedestal.

NATURAL ATTRACTIONS

The Indians said it was the "place where the clouds are born," and they called it *Iguassú,* meaning "mighty waters." Later visitors have called Iguazú Falls, between Argentina and Brazil, the "most stupendous spectacle in South America." Here the waters of the mighty Iguazú River plunge with a stupendous roar into breathtaking Devil's Throat Canyon. The river tumbles in a broken series of cataracts over a ledge some two and a half miles wide, into a gorge more than two hundred feet below. The smaller portion of the falls is on the Argentine side.

Today, thousands of tourists visit the falls. There are fine hotels on both the Argentine and Brazilian sides, and Argentina has made its part of the region a national park covering 133,000 acres.

Another world-famous natural wonder of Argentina is the Puento del Inca natural bridge, about a hundred miles from Mendoza. The natural bridge looms more than sixty feet above the Mendoza River and stretches about seventy feet.

Not so well known, but the favorite of many international travelers, is Lanín volcano, said by some to be more lovely than Mt. Fujiyama in Japan. Located in the heart of the great lakes region of Argentina which stretches along much of the mountain border country, it is considered one of the finest mountain vacation centers anywhere.

Most visitors claim that the lakes region more than lives up to its reputation as the "Switzerland of South America." Some visitors claim it is far more beautiful than Switzerland. Nahuel Huapí National Park is the best known of the seven national parks and one reservation, all extending southward along the Chilean border.

In the heart of the park lies famed Lake Nahuel Huapí, meaning "Island of the Tiger" in the Pampa Indian language. The long deep arms of this lake extend like fjords into the arms of the mountains, with its forty-mile-long surface a sparkling canvas of purples, greens, and blues, surrounded everywhere by the snowy peaks of the Cordillera range of the Andes. One of the best-known hotels in Argentina is the Llao Llao on the shores of Lake Nahuel Huapí. On the sides of El Tronador Mountain (the Thunderer), glaciers gleam and drop their icebergs with mighty crashes into the chilly waters of the lake.

The quaint town of Bariloche is the gateway to the park and the headquarters for tourists. In winter skiing is very popular on these world-famous ski slopes. In summer, fishing, hiking, mountaineering, horseback riding, boating, and motoring are all popular. At the Forest Research Station on Victoria Island, tame guanacos and deer roam, and rare plants grow.

In Bariloche, the Francisco P. Moreno Museum, named in honor of the famous

naturalist who persuaded the government to make the region a national park to preserve its beauties for all time, exhibits relics from the region's Indians.

While the other national parks and lakes are not so well known as Nahuel Huapí, their magnificent scenery and other attractions draw an ever-increasing number of visitors.

Southernmost of the national parks is Tierra del Fuego National Park, on the strange and forbidding island where the world's next-to-most-southerly city, Ushuaia, is located. Here glaciers flow down to the sea to "calve" their icebergs into the ocean traffic lanes.

From the forbidding vastness of Tierra del Fuego to the cosmopolitan glamour of Buenos Aires, Argentina displays its vast range of attractions—a land beloved by its energetic people who have just begun to use the potential of their country.

Handy Reference Section

INSTANT FACTS

Political:

Official Name—Republic of Argentina

Capital—Buenos Aires

Monetary Unit—Peso (one hundred centavos equal one peso)

Official Language—Spanish

Official Religion—Roman Catholic (required of president and vice-president only, though practiced by about eighty-four percent of the people)

Flag—Three horizontal stripes of equal width; middle one white with golden sun in center; other two light blue. Sun represents the "Sun of May," symbol of independence.

National Flower—Ceibo

Geographical:

Area—1,074,745 square miles

Greatest Length (north to south)—2,295 miles

Greatest Width (east to west)—980 miles

Highest Point—22,834 ft. (Mt. Aconcagua)

Lowest Point—131 ft. below sea level (Peninsula Valdes)

HOLIDAYS

National Holidays:

May 1—Labor Day

May 25—Revolution of May, 1810

June 20—Flag Day

July 9—Argentine Independence, 1816

August 17—Anniversary of the death of San Martín

October 12—Day of the Race

December 25—Christmas

POPULATION

Population History:

1950	17,070,000
1955	18,900,000
1960	20,005,691
1968	23,500,000 (estimate)

Population Distribution—68% urban; 32% rural

Birth Rate per 1,000—21.5

Death Rate per 1,000—8.2

Average Life-span—66 years

Literacy Rate—91%

Principal Cities:

Buenos Aires (Greater)	6,735,000 (1968 estimate)
Rosario	595,000
Córdoba	580,000
La Plata (Greater)	410,000

Population of Provinces (1960 Census):

Province	Population	Capital City
Buenos Aires	6,734,548	La Plata
Catamarca	172,407	Catamarca
Chaco	535,443	Resistencia
Chubut	142,195	Rawson
Córdoba	1,759,997	Córdoba
Corrientes	543,226	Corrientes
Entre Rios	803,505	Paraná
Formosa	178,458	Formosa
Jujuy	239,783	Jujuy
La Pampa	158,489	Santa Rosa
La Rioja	128,270	La Rioja
Mendoza	825,535	Mendoza
Misiones	391,094	Posadas
Neuquén	111,008	Neuquén
Rio Negro	192,595	Viedma
Salta	412,652	Salta
San Juan	352,461	San Juan
San Luis	174,251	San Luis
Santa Cruz	52,853	Río Gallegos
Santa Fe	1,865,537	Santa Fe
Santiago del Estero	477,156	Santiago del Estero
Tucumán	780,348	Tucumán
Tierra del Fuego (Territory)	7,064	Ushuaia
Buenos Aires (Federal District)	2,966,816	

CLIMATE

	Average Summer Temperature	Average Winter Temperature	Average Yearly Rainfall
North	77°F	55°F	40-60 inches
Central	74°F	49°F	20-30
South	70°F	35°F	3-16

Average temperature in Buenos Aires—61°F

YOU HAVE A DATE WITH HISTORY

1516—Juan Díaz de Solís discovers the Río de la Plata
1520—Ferdinand Magellan discovers Strait of Magellan
1526—Sebastian Cabot explores
1536—Pedro de Mendoza starts first settlement at Buenos Aires (later abandoned)
1553—Oldest permanent city, Santiago del Estero, founded
1561—Mendoza founded
1562—San Juan founded
1565—Tucumán founded
1573—Córdoba founded
1580—Buenos Aires refounded
1588—Corrientes founded
1591—La Rioja founded
1593—Jujuy founded
1602—Poet Centenera first uses name of Argentina
1613—University of Córdoba founded by Jesuits
1617—First Jesuit mission founded
1767—All Jesuits ordered out of Argentina
1776—Viceroyalty of the Río de la Plata created
1778—José de San Martín born
1806—English capture Buenos Aires; then forced out
1810—Junta takes over rule in name of deposed king
1816—Independence proclaimed at Tucumán
1817—San Martín and Army of the Andes cross mountains, liberate Chile
1821—University of Buenos Aires founded
1835—Juan Manuel de Rosas becomes dictator
1850—San Martín dies in France
1852—Rosas overcome in Battle of Caseros
1853—Constitution adopted, first president elected
1857—First railroad opened for use
1865—War with Paraguay begins
1880—Revolution establishes Buenos Aires as Federal District
1883—Julio A. Roca completes conquest of Indians
1897—Mount Aconcagua first climbed
1907—Petroleum industry begun
1912—Law enacted creating secret ballot and compulsory voting
1916—First free national elections
1919—"Tragic Week" of labor troubles
1932—Greatest highway building period begins
1946—Juan Perón elected President
1951—First television broadcasts
1955—Perón deposed
1958—Dr. Arturo Frondizi elected President
1962—Military overthrows Frondizi
1963—Dr. Arturo Illía elected President
1966—Military overthrows Dr. Illía; Juan Carlos Ongania heads government
1968—Argentina becomes eligible for membership in International Monetary Fund

SPECIAL EVENTS

January—Wheat Harvest Festival, Santa Fe and San Genaro Norte
January—Traditional Festival, San Juan
February—Feast of Pacha Mama (Mother Earth), northern region
February—Carnival, La Rioja and Jujuy
February—Wool Festival, Santa Cruz
February—Festival of the Sellers, Mar del Plata
February—Tourist Celebration, San Luis
March—Grape (Bacchus) Festival, Mendoza
March—International Festival of the Cine (Film Festival), Mar del Plata
March—International Regatta, Buenos Aires
March—Wheat Harvest Festival, Córdoba
April—Festival of the Virgin of the Valley, Catamarca
April—Apple Harvest Celebration, Rio Negro and Neuquén
April—Holy Week Procession, Tandil
April—National Olive Festival, Córdoba
May—The Week of La Rioja, La Rioja
May 25—1810 Revolution, nationwide
June—Feast of St. Peter, Tucumán
June—Argentine Cinema Festival, Santiago del Estero
June—Saltanian Week, Salta
June—National Flag Day, Santa Fe
July—National Cattle Show, Buenos Aires (Federal District)
July—Welsh Festival, Chubut
July—Week of St. Ann, Jujuy
July 9—Independence Day, nationwide
August—International Skiing Championships and Snow Festival, Bariloche
August—Pilgrimage to the "Pacercitas," La Rioja
August—Snow Festival, Mendoza
August—Jujuy Week, Jujuy
August—Santiago del Estero Week, Santiago del Estero
August—International Folklore Festival, Santiago del Estero
August—San Luis Week, San Luis
August—Catamarca Week, Catamarca
September—Festival of Our Lord, Salta
September—Skiing Championship, Neuquén
September 21—Student Day, nationwide
October—Feast of the Pots and Pans, Jujuy
October—Sugar Festival, Tucumán
October—Gran Premio Turf Races, Buenos Aires (Federal District)
November—Strawberry Festival, Santa Fe
November—Day of Tradition, Buenos Aires
November—Carlos Pellegrini Race, Buenos Aires
November—Festival of the Monkey Nut, Córdoba
November—Santa Fe Week, Santa Fe
December—Mar del Plata Week, Mar del Plata
December—International Fishing Contest, Neuquén

INDEX

95